# Organising Successful Learning Events

A guide to planning and running conferences, seminars and workshops for anyone involved in facilitating training in the people-services

## Alan Dearling

**RHP**

Russell House Publishing

First published in 1992 by Longman under the title
*How to Organise Conferences, Workshops and Training Events*

This substantially revised and updated version published in 2003 as *Organising Successful Learning Events* by:
Russell House Publishing Ltd.
4 St. George's House
Uplyme Road
Lyme Regis
Dorset DT7 3LS

Tel: 01297-443948
Fax: 01297-442722
e-mail: help@russellhouse.co.uk
www.russellhouse.co.uk

© Alan Dearling

British Library Cataloguing-in-publication Data:
A catalogue record for this book is available from the British Library.

ISBN: 1-903855-33-0

Design and layout by Jeremy Spencer. Cover illustration by Wayne Chung.

Printed by Cromwell Presss, Trowbridge.

---

**About Russell House Publishing**

RHP is a group of social work, probation, education and youth and community work practitioners and academics working in collaboration with a professional publishing team. Our aim is to work closely with the field to produce innovative and valuable materials to help managers, trainers, practitioners and students.
We are keen to receive feedback on publications and new ideas for future projects.
For details of our other publications please visit our website or ask us for a catalogue.
Contact details are on this page.

# Contents

v

# Preface

This book is essentially an up-dated version of a book I compiled for publication by Longman in 1992, which was later marketed by Pavilion Publishing. I thank my colleagues and friends at Russell House Publishing for asking me to review and renew its contents.

It is very much a cumulative, co-operative effort. I have tried to consolidate in one place much of the training and conference experience which I have gained in the past thirty years of working in, and for, youth and community work departments; schools; colleges and universities; social work and housing agencies; charities and voluntary organisations, and the publishing and journalistic industries. All these environments have contributed to the materials presented in this book. There is no clear process of underlining I can do to differentiate between those examples of training and conference planning and practice that are 'mine', and those which I have observed, borrowed, amended, or been a partner in. Where possible I have acknowledged sources for examples I have used from published works.

Mistakes I've made along the way are obviously mine (!), but I would like to say an especial 'thank you' to colleagues from a range of organisations for sharing their knowledge and skills with me. Some of the organisations are still going strong; some have faded in the mists of time or evolved into new agencies. In recent times I've worked particularly with the Chartered Institute of Housing, London School of Economics, Brunel and Goldsmiths' universities, Social Work in Europe journal, the University of Luton and the University of Wales College at Cardiff and the youth service in and around the border of Dorset and Devon.

In earlier 'lives' I did a lot of work with colleagues from Shelter, Save the Children, NSPCC, NCH Action for Children, NITFed, NACRO, NAYJ, NYA (previously the National Youth Bureau), Queen's College, Langdale College and Jordanhill College, all in Glasgow; Apex Trust, the Community and Youth Workers' Union and the NUT, Youth and Policy, the Scottish Intermediate Treatment Training Group and their memorable annual conference and Scottish training 'roadshows', Moray House College in Edinburgh and the Institute of Education in London.

Finally, on a personal note, I'd like to express my appreciation for the advice and professional comradeship I have received in my training work from Alan Taylor, now of Home Office, Trevor Locke, previously with NACRO, and Howie Armstrong, Kevin Gill, Tim Pickles and Bruce Britton who I worked with in our 'bit' of the Scottish Office empire. Also, I'm indebted to friends like Kate Whitehorn, Cat Martin, Lois Johnson, Douglas Robertson, Alan Marlow, John Pitts, Geraldine Peacock, Tim Newburn, Phil Bayliss, Tony Jeffs, Philip Hope (currently an MP, rather than trainer), Alison Nimmo and her partner Jeremy Wyatt, and Frank Booton, who is sadly no longer with us.

I could make this into an endless list, but suffice it to say a 'thank you' to every one else who has trained, conferenced or workshopped with me...

Happy training and learning!
**Alan Dearling**

# Glossary

There are certain words which have crept into the English language which belong to the twin worlds of training and the caring services. Not everyone knows what they mean, nor does everybody share the same meanings. Below is my attempt to briefly define some of the words used in this book. In some cases, fuller definitions are offered in the main part of the book, in others, you may find my definitions a bit quirky, but hopefully helpful!

**Animateur:** is the name for a facilitator in training who stresses empowerment and enabling of participants and learners.

**Audio-visual aids:** are the range of equipment which can be used in training to enhance presentations or improve learning. They include audio tapes; tape-slide shows; video, computer and television presentations; overhead projection; film and lighting equipment.

**Brainstorming:** is a technique where a facilitator invites quick comments, ideas and responses to a specific problem or topic. It is often used to promote creativity in a group, and the trick is for the facilitator to accept all the ideas offered and write them up on a flip-chart or board for later analysis and discussion. It is a central method for stimulating group activity in group work (which is a structured method of empowering individuals, and promoting team and group cohesion through shared experiences and activity).

**Case studies:** are examples of realistic practice from workers' experience. They can be presented either as written accounts, or verbally by a facilitator.

**Casework/care work:** these two terms have become rather confused with the implementation of community care strategies. The idea is that social workers and others involved in social care should work with clients to tailor care packages to meet individual needs.

**Cluster or buzz groups:** are usually groups of between three and about eight participants, who are invited by an event organiser or session leader to form up for a short period of time, five to fifteen minutes at the most. The group will usually have a task to perform, or a subject to discuss. The idea is to promote participation and stimulate the flow of ideas.

**Community care:** is the umbrella term which is used (and abused) to describe a positive strategy for the development of domiciliary, day and respite services which enable people to live in their own homes, wherever feasible. It is also used to describe services which offer consumers and carers: flexible and sensitively provided services; more choice and options; intervention which fosters independence, and positive discrimination for those with the greatest needs.

**Competence(s) (ies):**   the adoption of work-place assessment for many social care and health staff, and increasingly for part-time workers in community education, has led to the wider use of 'competence' as measure of a person's ability to perform a task, use a particular piece of equipment or master a skill. More and more training is being designed to assist staff in developing competencies in different areas of their working practices.

**Conference:**   this is the rather grand name for special kinds of larger meetings, which may involve training, debate, discussion and a whole range of learning and teaching techniques. Most social care and education conferences last between one and five days, and are usually 'one-off' events arranged around a theme, area of common concern or specialist professional grouping. They may or may not involve overnight accommodation.

**Consumers:**   since the late 1980s, the people who use health, social work, housing and education/community support facilities and services have been seen as active partners, who should be at very least 'consulted'. In training events, consumers are more frequently invited to participate as 'equals' alongside professionals and volunteer staff. The terms 'user', 'client' and 'customer' are also used in the various caring services.

**Co-working:**   is a method used in training where two trainers or facilitators work together in a partnership to present training sessions. The main benefits are that it gives greater diversity in terms of presentational styles and information, and allows the trainers to test ideas and support one another.

**Critical incident analysis:**   is a training technique which involves participants looking in detail at specific incidents from their work which were worrying, which caused problems, or which were not satisfactorily resolved. The training aim is to encourage participants to look at options, to gain confidence and to be in a position to work more effectively in the future.

**Debate, forum, panel:**   these are forms of plenary or relatively large-scale meeting, where a structured discussion is organised. Often, particular people with different backgrounds or points of view are invited by the organisers, at an event, to share their opinions and perceptions with the other participants.

**Discussion groups:**   these normally have a facilitator who helps get the group to focus on a subject and may have prepared a set of questions in advance. As in workshops, they may be required to feedback material to a larger group if the discussion group is a part of a bigger event.

**e-Learning:**   on the Internet there is a wide range of opportunities for individuals to become involved in discussion groups and information exchange. Sending an e-mail and receiving a reply is the most basic exchange. Increasingly, there are Internet-based learning courses being run for learners on the web. These can lead to accreditation by organisations such as the Open University.

**Empowerment:** is a very fashionable phrase. Training work can sometimes be frightening and potentially 'de-skill' staff by making the activity too threatening. Empowerment through training means shifting power, control and decision-making away from the 'trainers' and into the community of the participants and the trainers. Partnership working is another term used to describe this relationship between providers and consumers.

**Exercises:** these are organised sequences designed to aid involvement, enable participants to focus on tasks, and sometimes to learn new skills and information. Some take the form of games or simulations, which are either fun ways of learning or sharing, or a way of re-creating a situation as a learning experience. They may be co-operative, group oriented, or individual and competitive.

**Experiential learning:** is what it sounds like; learning based on personal experience, and learning which effectively involves and is 'owned' by the participants.

**Focus groups:** training is often used to inform and improve practice. Focus groups are structured groups of people, chosen by age, gender, behaviour, attitude, beliefs or some other particular characteristic such as ethnicity. They may be consulted for their particular views on a problem or potential solution. Focus groups are used frequently in qualitative research to act as a test bed for ideas and changes that are occurring during a particular study.

**Ice-breakers:** are particular types of games and training sequences designed to promote involvement, activity and break down the inhibitions of participants.

**Learning objectives:** are established for particular training or pieces of work. They are usually worded in ways which make them assessable, clear, and possible to monitor. They can be very useful when established for training which it is important to measure in terms of successful outcomes and effectiveness.

**Learning organisations:** these are agencies that have decided to proactively make efforts to empower all their staff to take advantage of training and professional development opportunities on offer. They tend to see learning as an essential element of continuing or lifelong education.

**Lectures:** are usually up to an hour in length and may be given by one or more speakers, usually based on previously prepared notes. They are a form of speech, and the 'keynote' speech or lecture at a conference usually highlights the main theme or subject area for the whole event. Sometimes they are followed by the opportunity for those who have listened to ask the speaker questions afterwards. They are the most formal part of training events and involve participants passively receiving information and views.

**Multi-disciplinary/ multi-agency work:** more and more professional groups and different organisations are being encouraged to form teams to work together. Since they do not necessarily share the same 'discipline' of training, or the same shared knowledge and language, training in multi-disciplinary teams needs to address this as part of the process of learning. Multi-agency work brings different statutory and voluntary agencies into working partnerships, with the intention of better co-ordination and collaboration in pursuit of better services for the consumer.

**Needs assessment:** assessing needs is a prioritising task which takes place in most 'people-work'. In its professionalised sense, it means making the best judgement of what actions are required to remedy disadvantages in social and economic life. An assessment can be made for an individual, a community or even for a service organisation. In training, 'needs' are often the heading chosen by facilitators to start discussion, as a way of analysing situations and potential options for responses. 'Training needs' are often part of the list which managers build up with their staff. Individuals will usually have personal training needs, in addition to training needs which they have as part of the organisation or team.

**Networks/networking:** are a major component in community care strategies and are a method of work organisation. Networking implies actively establishing links between different providers, carers and service users. Often there will be both 'formal' and 'informal' networks in operation. In training, 'networks' of consultants and trainers are often established to ensure that skills can be exchanged and made available on a needs basis.

**Normalisation:** is a process which is being used increasingly to try and help devalued people gain or regain respect, self-confidence and in general improve the quality of their lives. Normalisation can be seen as a form of training, which helps overcome prejudices and discrimination, and which can remove the stigma which is often attached to 'people' when they are dehumanised through the services which label them as 'patients', 'clients', 'ill', 'offenders', 'insane', 'unemployed', 'handicapped' or whatever.

**People-work/people-services:** are the terms I've used in this book to cover all the professions and organisations who work in the range of the personal social services. In the UK this covers social work; education; probation; youth and community work; housing; work with offenders and health.

**Plenary:** this is the name given to meetings in training events and conferences which are attended by all the participants. Some plenaries feature a speaker, or series of speakers; others offer the opportunity for debate, and some plenaries are used to sum up and review the proceedings of a conference or event.

| | |
|---|---|
| **Professional development:** | a potentially diverse range of learning opportunities, undertaken in different situations. Overall, if applied as a conscious system, it can offer a range of ways to improve skills and knowledge. |
| **Quality assurance/ quality management:** | are umbrella management terms which are being embodied in many 'people-work' services to describe the adoption of 'whole organisation' strategies for improving the quality of services through better communication; more sensitive and empowering consumer care; improvements in co-ordination and monitoring of work; improved training and planning. Much team and organisational training is taking place as a means of developing total quality management. |
| **Rapporteur:** | is the name given to the person who is often attached to a workshop or group session and makes notes or a record of key points coming out of the group interaction and discussion. The rapporteur will usually report back either to the group itself, or to the larger group meeting. |
| **Role-plays:** | involve participants acting out different roles and re-creating situations which can be analysed in terms of what happened – why – and what can be learned from the different roles people play in real life situations. |
| **Seminars:** | these traditionally involve one or more people making a presentation that is then discussed by the other members of the seminar group. Much used in academic institutions, the seminar usually lasts between one hour and two and a half hours, and has between five and fifteen members. |
| **Trainer, tutor, facilitator, organiser, enabler and animateur:** | are all terms used in training circles to describe the person who organises or leads a training session. Facilitation, animation and enabling are all seen as positive and creative ways of working with trainees, using sharing and partnership techniques. |
| **Training event:** | these can come in all shapes and sizes. A conference can be one form of training event. Likewise, seminars, workshops and some courses can be called 'training events'. |
| **Workshops:** | the name implies activity and participation. Usually they have a leader or facilitator, who determines the style and content of the workshop. Often they are arranged around tasks, themes or special interests, and a workshop group may be asked to produce a group consensus, written or verbal statement. They vary in length and size, but are normally at least an hour and a half long, and may sometimes provide the base for a group of staff or participants to meet regularly over a long period of time. |

# Introduction

The effectiveness of work in social welfare, health, care, housing and education sectors – the **people-services** – depends to a great extent upon the provision of the 'best possible' training and support for staff. There is no right or wrong way to organise training or encourage continuing education and learning. Each conference, training event, workshop or seminar is different – unique to the people, place, time and subject under consideration. However, there are now many occasions where almost every member of staff will be expected to actively assist in the preparation, planning and running of different types of training and personal professional development.

This book is a modest attempt to provide practical and relevant material that has been gained from 'coal face' experience. No one trainer or training event organiser can, in any way, claim to 'own' the answers to the very best ways to put together a training package or a conference. A lot will depend on the nitty-gritty of how much funding and time is available for staff to meet together, the availability of a suitable venue, experienced and motivated facilitators, and good planning and preparation.

The material included throughout this book should help to build the confidence and skills of even the very new trainer or staff group entrusted with the task of planning and organising any sort of training or learning event. Using the variety of materials and ideas they should be able to get on with the task in hand, hopefully minimising some of the mistakes along the learning curve!

What I've provided is a mixture of **administrative checklists and forms** that should help to focus tasks, and allow for the best allocation and division of jobs, and a range of **planning materials and ideas**, which should assist any training planning group to clarify their thoughts as to:

- What they are trying to achieve?
- Why is the training event, programme or conference being held?
- Who is it for?
- What sort of programme will achieve these objectives?
- What styles of training or learning are most appropriate?
- What practical issues are involved e.g. for marketing the event, accommodation, administration, engaging speakers and workshop leaders etc.?
- What equipment and resource needs are there?
- What follow-up and evaluation is required?

This list can obviously be extended almost infinitely, but these are the bare bones of the structure for organising training. What makes the conferences, training events and workshops in the broad network of people-services rather different from those planned for the commercial and industrial worlds is that in commerce the aims are more likely to be geared towards maximising productivity and profit. In the people-services they are usually geared towards **improving services, empowering user groups and customers, improving staff and consumer skills and confidence, and combating inequalities**. The new meeting place between the two cultures is in ensuring **'quality assurance'**, **'competencies'** and **'best value'** of services.

Throughout this book, these aims will be reinforced, since training and staff development in the social welfare and education services must be focused on the provision of learning opportunities which build on personal experience and which meet the needs of the communities and individuals that they are serving. This interfaces quality assurance with welfare principles, and systems approaches with individual and personal development needs. So, while a lot of this book is concerned with improving organisational practices, the emphasis is very much on doing so within the context of partnership working between those being trained and trainers, multi-disciplinary groups of workers, and qualified and unqualified staff and their consumers.

In addition to the staff development aspect of training in the people-services, there will be some events which are aimed at the media, or the consumers/customers. Increasingly, conferences and events are held as part of the strategic effort by organisations and groups of workers to 'sell' a message, or a way of working. Or, the event may be intended to make other people aware of particular innovations or problems, such as in work with drug or alcohol abusers, AIDS sufferers, child sexual abuse, mental health initiatives, homelessness, or implementing the curriculum changes in schools.

We must also be aware that raising income through 'consciousness-raising' can often be a major aim in conferences, where the continued existence of an organisation, type of work or even profession, may depend upon influencing the planners, funders and decision-makers. In these instances, a conference may be seen as part of the campaigning strategy, and its success or otherwise must be measured by different criteria, not just the provision of learning opportunities. For instance, a campaign event might be seen as a success if it attracts certain levels of media attention or new members to the organisation.

Most of the material collected together in this book has been assembled the 'hard way'. Colleagues and myself have made plenty of mistakes (and will continue to do so!) in the process of putting on 'best possible' training. But, equally, we have learned some useful lessons and insights, often through confronting problems. You can learn a lot when you are organising a 400-person conference in a rambling, Gothic hotel just before Christmas on an island off the west of Scotland. Suddenly you hear by telephone that your main speaker's plane, the last of the day, has failed to take off from East Midlands' airport, and your delegates are expecting a 'keynote' speech after dinner at 8 o'clock. Shades of 'Fawlty Towers', but a not-too-unlikely scenario for any would-be training event organisers! In the event, the organising committee had an emergency meeting, and they provided an instant, warts-'n'-all presentation themselves on *Ways forward in community-based child care*. Because it was 'for real', passionate, and based on the everyday experience of the managers and fieldwork staff involved, it was probably better received than the planned presentational overview from a university-based academic.

Much of training and conference planning should be viewed as a challenge and an adventure. And in the worlds of the voluntary and statutory agencies working in the various sectors of social welfare and education, the events must be as much about partnership working, sharing and empowering as we can possibly make them.

**Any training event is principally a forum for the exchange of experience, skills, information and opinions, and each event must be sensitive to the backgrounds of the participants, the particular characteristics of the specialist subject or profession involved, as well as being organised to meet the overall aims of the event.**

Training and education opportunities exist for a variety of purposes. The range is enormous. Personal and professional development are at the heart of most of them. In social welfare type of work that is most likely to mean providing opportunities for staff to **gain skills to do their jobs more effectively or to provide improved services**.

Some events and training offer some form of 'accreditation'; others are primarily opportunities for staff (and possibly their clients or customers) to get together and debate practice and policy. NVQs are an example of staged accreditation. They utilise the credit accumulation system and offer opportunities for unqualified or relatively poorly qualified staff in social welfare jobs, to work up the ladder of credits, moving from one level of award to the next as a natural progression. Each 'award' is a stage in the process of becoming 'trained' or 'qualified'.

The idea of a beginning, a middle, and an end, is a familiar and commonsense one to all who have ever been cajoled into writing an essay, a book or thesis. Planning for training or conference events is essentially a matter of establishing stages for the process. Within a single event, even a relatively simple one, such as a half-day induction training session for new staff joining a local authority or voluntary organisation, a number of people may have been involved in the:

- planning
- administration
- co-ordination
- presentation
- evaluation and follow-up

The event itself may be a 'stand-alone' affair, or part of a series of workshops, a structured course or an accreditation mechanism leading specifically to assessment and qualification. In the organisation of conferences, workshops and training events, the 'getting started' phase is of vital importance. If the planner or planning group haven't thought things through, some of the 'organisational variables' may get overlooked. This inevitably leads to recriminations, conflict and potentially both lost opportunities and loss of money and effectiveness. Any training event is **an opportunity**. The opportunity will have boundaries and constraints. There will also be potential areas where things can go a little or a lot wrong. It is the job of the event organisers to take on board the task of overseeing all the stages; that is the beginning, the middle, and the end!

## And in the beginning...

At the outset, the planning for any potential event may be assessed using a checklist of questions which will help to focus attention on what the group or trainer wants to achieve, how best to meet identified aims, what resources will be required, and an appropriate programme and timetable.

The first question is:

*Why is an event going to be organised?*

Any organiser, or organising group needs to discuss how best to tackle this question. Often it is not as straightforward as it may at first appear. 'Training' is usually seen as a 'good thing' in most organisations, but in the social care and education arenas, as much as anywhere else, it can be easy to provide events on the basis of a 'wing and a prayer'. To organise events and training effectively and efficiently, Hugh Koch has said in *Total Quality Management in Health Care* that training in quality must satisfy the following requirements:

- Unit level managers must be committed and involved in planning and setting training priorities.
- Objectives must be adequately and realistically resourced and timetabled.
- Training should be considered for all parts and levels of the provider unit.

This is a whole organisation, or 'holistic' approach to training, and holds equally true, in a modified form, for conferences and events which are not seen specifically as training, but have essentially the same structure. There is also an element of the 'chicken and egg' problem involved; is it better to try and define a programme for an event first and then 'sell' it to the intended audience? Or, should the audience be consulted as part of the process? In Hugh's example, taken from the world of health management, it is seen as fundamental that management would support and 'own' a commitment to planned training. This is equally important in any other 'people-services' training or conference, though it may be policy-makers, planners or the members of a housing estate, who need to be seen as involved and committed to the particular event being planned.

It is worth looking in a bit more detail, at how asking a series of questions about the intention and aims of an event can help to define the priorities for the planners. Perhaps too often in the past, some organisers for events have sat around in a classic social work or education circle of chairs and made some very rash assumptions at the very beginning of the planning stage for a conference or training event. For instance, it is relatively common for national steering groups and specialist professional groups to have a conference sub-group. Their accountability is to the main organisation, which may, in turn, be elected under some sort of process – often in a show of hands or ballot at the annual conference, which the sub-group is selected from, or co-opted to. In its worst excess, this group can become a self-perpetuating example of too much power being delegated to a non-representative, marginal grouping.

## Why is an event going to be organised?

Any group should, at the outset, ask itself questions such as those in Checklist 1.1 (see page 11). If you are planning to organise an event, Checklist 1.1, at the end of this section, may be worth considering for modification, **as a starting point for planning a conference, workshop or training event**.

If a **planning group or organiser** works out the answers to the Checklist 1.1 questions, these will provide the essential brief for the event and the beginning of a programme. Any organiser(s) must have decided on the objectives before trying to work out the content. Discussing the aim of an event and the objectives can be stimulated by taking some **buzz words** and seeing if they can be used to stimulate the most appropriate set of objectives. One set I generated with a conference planning group included the words (in relation to objectives for participants):

- interest
- involve
- inform
- educate
- stimulate
- entertain
- engage
- professionalise

- challenge
- practical
- theory
- participate
- make controversial
- generate new ideas
- innovation

A different planning group might create a very different list of objectives. It is worth considering the creation of such a list to form the basis for a short **planning exercise** for the organising group. The questions in Checklist 1.2 (see page 12) take the conference or event organiser into a second stage of detail.

In people-work services, training events and conferences increasingly use fewer information-giving sessions, and rather more exchanges of information. Participants are encouraged to participate, exchange views and to use their **experiential** knowledge, based on their own personal life experiences. This makes them much more **active** rather than **passive** in the conduct, and indeed in the planning of training type events. To enable this style of event, the organisers must:

- Brief all session organisers and workshop leaders on preferred 'styles' of presentation.
- Indicate in any briefing notes that sessions should be participative and experiential.
- Make training inputs as relevant to participants as possible and provide experiences and exercises which are challenging, but also supportive and non-judgemental.
- Provide opportunities to build up the confidence and skills of participants.

## Consultation and planning

At the planning stage, the scale and format of the event may determine some of the practical requirements for the planning group or event organiser.

The complexity of the tasks facing the planning group will be one of the variables for consideration based on a number of factors, such as those set out in Checklist 1.3 (see page 13).

# Aims and goals

Because the range of aims and goals for conferences and training events is so varied, it is not possible for me to emphasise too strongly the need to determine these at an early stage. Checklist 1 offered some of the aims for training events. The list below is based on the work of Leonard Nadler: *The Conference Book* and Burke and Beckhard: *Conference Planning*.

Training events and related conferences assume that in the process of training, or reflecting on work 'away from base', participants should be given opportunities to leave their normal work and domestic worlds and enter the world of the event. Depending upon the nature of the event, for instance, whether it is the conference of a professional association in probation, or a one-day in-service course for housing staff on the implications of community care in a local area, the participants should be encouraged to assist in:

• The rule setting for the event (either before or during the event).
• Setting objectives for the event.
• Determining how follow-up can be organised.
• The planning and co-ordination of the event.
• Choosing the programme, venue and contributors.

There is also a growing need to assess whether training is best achieved 'away from base' or in the workplace. Increasingly, especially in training for qualifications, training takes place in a mixture of locations. Training events should reinforce workplace on-the-job training, and should be clearly relevant to the needs of both individuals and organisations back in the workplace. Like many people, who have been involved in putting training events together, we all remember personal 'horror stories'. Many could be avoided if more active collaboration was encouraged between planners, trainers and participants (see Figure 1.1).

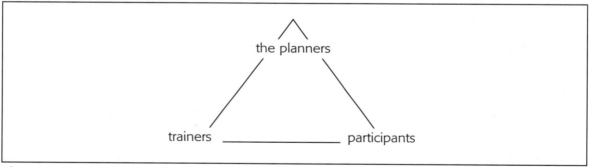

**Figure 1.1**

A salutory experience I well remember involved a planning group consisting of senior, well-intentioned staff from a major national voluntary child care organisation. They were planning a series of youth participation conferences, which were due to be launched at a national event. The trouble was that the members of the group were fearful that the young people would 'take over' and, in so doing, bring bad publicity to the sponsoring agency. In the event, a number of younger facilitators were invited to help run the sessions at the conference, and the organisers then quickly gave the power for the programme, and the running of the event, over to the young people. The initial distrust took a bit of overcoming, but the farther the original planning group moved into the background, the more successful the event became and, at the end of three days, all the participants were 'members' and 'citizens' of the event, and a lot of lively and challenging debate had taken place about power; relationships between young people and adults; sexism and racism, and how to avoid the original problems of organising the national conference. After the conference, many of the participants became the co-organisers of local events back in their own areas of the United Kingdom, and they put into practice the lessons learned about participation and collaboration. It does serve as a prime example of an event that lacked adequate consultation at the planning stages.

In more complex events, where many different types of 'interested parties' could be consulted, there may be conflicts of interest. These may not always be resolvable, but the process of consultation will usually do a lot to allay fears and encourage the sense of involvement and 'ownership' over the particular event. Burke and Beckhard take the view that the most fruitful model of participant is one who is:

> **a learner** *(an active participant)*

They contrast this model of participation with two other, less productive, forms of involvement, which they have called:

> **a tourist** *(a non-participant)*
>
> **an expatriate** *(uncritical consumer)*

In most of our people-work training events, the aims will reflect a mixture of intended benefits. You may wish to organise a short planning exercise based on Checklist 1.4 (see page 14) to look at the benefits of any event you are planning.

Looking at an event or piece of training in this way may help to determine the 'optimal' balance within a programme to meet the varying needs of organisation and individuals; the personal and professional development needs of staff, and the needs of consumers who are participating.

It may also be used to help in the process of consultation with other interested parties, by focusing the attention of those advising the planning group in areas which are likely to be constructive and positive for all concerned.

To wind up the consideration of how best to improve the planning stage, the model in Figure 1.2 may give an idea of all the people who might be consulted about the organisation and functioning of any particular event. This is not the same as saying that they *must* be contacted, but the more they can be involved at some stage, the greater the likelihood of your getting more learners and less tourists amongst the participants. It is also likely to offer something of a protection strategy for the planning group against those other famous groups:

> **the snipers** *(those who are wise after the event and say 'I told you so...')*
>
> **the whingers** *(those who do little but peevishly complain)*

No model of this kind can totally reflect the world of someone else's training event or conference – use it to **build up a model** which does describe the kind of event which you are planning.

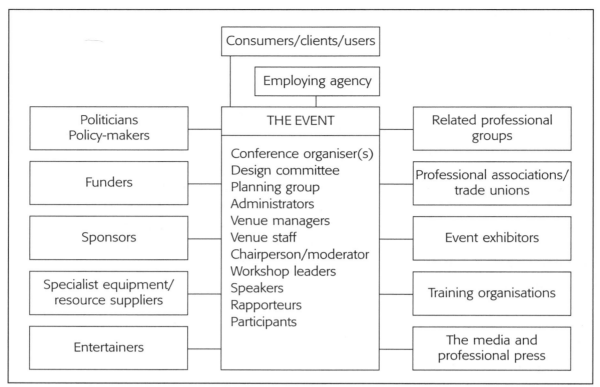

**Figure 1.2: A model of all those who are likely to be involved and might be consulted regarding a training event**

## Ground rules for training events

In commerce and industry, there has been a tendency for training to be closely linked with appraisal and assessment. In people-work, the last decades of the twentieth century saw a move towards a sharpening of focus, whereby staff and agencies were held increasingly accountable for expenditure and provision of services, not just to funders, administrators and politicians, but also to the consumers. Patients in the health service are now aware of the national charter standards and some of these seem appropriate as aims for 'empowerment', and could also be curiously appropriate for all participants in training events as a set of **ground rules**. In a slightly modified form, these could read as in Checklist 1.5 (see page 15).

In practice, a set of ground rules or **safeguards** should be developed by any planning group in training or training and conference organisers. These need to protect the participants from training being used as an instrument of oppression, and to positively challenge behaviour in training which may be seen as discriminatory. A model of how to arrive at appropriate safeguards is offered in *Section 4: Styles of training event.*

## Evaluation and assessment

A greater accent on quality, and the increase in monitoring of training means that evaluation techniques should be built into the planning process of any training event, rather than being 'tacked on', as a kind of ill-fitting afterthought.

**Evaluation and monitoring** are a continuous process. They are at their most effective when aims and learning objectives are easily quantifiable – not always so easy in people-work. However, if the aims and objectives are considered more clearly at the outset, the level of success can be more clearly monitored. Indeed, it seems reasonable to establish a model for evaluation which also looks at the efficiency and effectiveness of the planning and preparation stages of training events. In this way, Checklist 1.6 (see page 16) shows what the model might look like.

Once again, it is a pretty obvious case of 'horses for courses'. What is suitable as a means of assessment for a staff training scheme for a very specific form of training such 'best practice in child protection', will need modifying drastically for a group planning a trade union, or delegate conference, where an agenda will determine the proposers, seconders, and voting structure for the event in a much more rigid fashion than with a relatively open-ended, participative workshop.

## Training, learning and qualifications

This book is meant to help anyone who may face the sometimes frightening, but often exciting and challenging task of organising some form of training event. At the wider, more macro-level, involvement may be largely an administrative job – making sure that all the stages of planning, preparation and implementation are carried through efficiently. Or, you may as an individual, be dealing with only one aspect of the event, the micro-level of the event organisation, possibly designing the programme, liaising with speakers and workshop leaders, or registration at the venue. On the other hand, you may be charged with the task of seeing where a particular training event 'fits' into the larger scheme of personal and professional staff development. This may require you to have to seek recognition and accreditation for the event and provide certificates for those who attend.

**Lifelong learning** has moved beyond being a slogan. More people are choosing to get involved in learning and training at different times in their lives. This is also associated with the move towards agencies re-inventing themselves as **learning organisations**, meaning that they see empowerment of staff through learning, as a major element of their **mission statement** or **aims**.

It is way beyond the scope of this book to offer guidance on the enormous and growing range of in-service, vocational, distance-learning, NVQ, degree and post-graduate training, and other options for staff in the people-services. What is known is that in the quest for 'quality' of service, longer training for professionals has been decreed to be necessary. Two year courses are being replaced by three-year degree-level courses, top-up specialist courses are increasingly being run, and nearly every aspect of working with people in welfare-type services is now associated with some sort of accreditation. In fact, the situation sometimes reaches almost farcical proportions, when, for instance, a part-time youth worker needs a life saving certificate to take a group of kids down to the beach to build sand castles!

# Trends in training

In the 2000s, new trends in training and patterns of staff development will inevitably have a knock-on effect in the way training events and conferences and workshops are planned and structured. Training to improve the competency of staff and achieve a more qualified workforce is one key element in this evolution. Distance learning, and training through the Internet and computer terminals and software programs, are one element of this.

The implementation of new policies and new social priorities often serve to direct the content of training. For instance, criminal and anti-social behaviour and the impact of drugs on society are 'shared problems' for almost everyone working in the wide range of welfare and educational services. New challenges arise. For example, many welfare agencies have to respond to the needs of refugees and asylum seekers. This gives rise to training on a bespoke-tailored or a needs-to-know basis. There are also fundamental aspects of 'good practice' that need to be embedded into all training. These include:

- equal opportunities
- health and safety
- anti-sexist, harassment and racist strategies

As a last **exercise**, the planning group may wish to consider Checklist 1.7 (see page 17). Add your own changes to it, and other trends in training that you can identify as specific to your own 'profession', 'team' or 'agency'. Then think about the ways this needs to be reflected in your approach to the organisation of training events.

# Checklist 1.1: Why is an event going to be organised?

■ Why are we organising an event?

■ Who is it aimed at?

■ What are we trying to achieve through the organisation of the event?

■ What type of event is it? For instance, is it about?:
  – communicating information
  – planning and policy-making
  – skills training
  – decision-making
  – assessment and testing
  – campaigning
  – raising consciousness
  – political agendas
  – team-building
  – resource allocation
  – dealing with change
  – legislation
  – improving service delivery
  – attitude or behaviour modification
  – assertiveness
  – confidence-building

■ Will the event need to be evaluated and how?

# Checklist 1.2: The next stage

■ Does the event need to have a theme?

■ Is a title important? What should it be?

■ What sort of programme is required?

■ What implications are there for the style; format; length; cost and timing of the conference/event?

■ How can this event be marketed to the audience?

■ What resource implications are there?

Think about the need for:

– funding requests and subsidies

– equipment

– geographical location and type of venue and accommodation

– personnel implications for: administration; speakers or workshop leaders

– rapporteurs, convenors, spokespersons, chairpersons

– are there any special needs requirements, for instance, for physically or mentally handicapped; parents with children; participants on income support or with transport restrictions?

# Checklist 1.3: Consultation

■  How many participants will there be? What is the duration of the event?

■  Is the event part of any longer series of training?

■  How many tasks can be identified for delegation/allocation to the planning group members?

■  Do other organisations and individuals need to be consulted at the planning stage?

■  Will the style, programme and venue for the event have any implications for the amount of work required?

Consultation at this planning stage may have a number of benefits for the organisers. It can help the team charged with putting on an event to:

–  Focus on the key aspects of the event and thereby get the 'shape' of the event right, and appropriate, for the intended participants.

–  Utilise the goodwill and expertise of more people, and help ultimately in creating a constituency of support for the event.

–  Check out if there is any competition or opposition to the proposed event.

–  Generate new ideas for the programme.

–  Identify specific 'problems' and/or subjects for inclusion.

## Checklist 1.4: Identifying benefits

■ How are the aims of the event going to bring:
  - Benefits for the organisation and service?
  - Benefits for staff teams or working units?
  - Benefits for individual staff?
  - Benefits for consumers?

# Checklist 1.5: Ground rules for training

Training should:

- Encourage respect for privacy, dignity and religious and cultural beliefs.
- Enable everyone, including people with special needs, to use the service.
- Allow freedom of access to information and records.

To these, I would suggest adding:

- Encourage all to participate, regardless of background, race, sexual orientation, job position, seniority or status.
- Assist in the resolution of workplace conflicts and disagreements.
- Encourage participants to 'be all they can be' and make the most of all training and staff development programmes.
- Relate to the actual practice in the workplace and provide opportunities to examine, evaluate and improve that practice.
- Be empowering and enabling, allowing, as far as possible, experiential approaches to be used.
- Establish learning objectives which explicitly and simply state what a participant will learn from particular learning modules, and which may be capable of being assessed.

# Checklist 1.6: Evaluation and monitoring

There are four stages of a training event or conference:

1.   The planning stage.

2.   Preparation for the event.

3.   During the event.

4.   After the event.

To some degree, in all of these four stages, there should be on-going evaluation as to how far:

—   Aims were established and met.

—   A transfer of knowledge and skills was accomplished.

—   Effective methods, styles and 'trainer' resources and inputs were utilised.

—   Needs were identified, met, and solutions implemented back in the workplace.

—   Potential areas for improving individual, team and organisational change and improvements have been recognised.

# Checklist 1.7: Training trends

Other **identifiable trends in training** which have evolved over the last 15-20 years include:

- More inter-disciplinary and multi-agency training.

- More modular training, which builds up credits, which may be transferable to higher level courses and qualifications.

- More training which includes a high level of on-the-job assessment of competencies and follows patterns established under City and Guilds and National Vocational Qualification awards.

- Pressure from government for a greater proportion of staff to have at least basic qualifications in social care and other forms of care, education and welfare work.

- More one-off courses offering specialist, rather than generic skills in areas such as counselling; financial and budgeting practice; information technology applications; resource management skills; specific legislation, etc.

- Increased use of courses and events as part of larger packages which include consultancy; supervision and assessment at the workplace; open and distance learning materials; appraisal schemes; monitoring systems using computer-based 'tracking' and use of such 'instruments' for assessment, such as performance indicators and client/patient trails.

- Involvement of more consumers in training events which 'empower' and encourage partnership working between staff in social welfare and education agencies and their different consumers, whether they are known as pupils and parents; patients; clients or customers.

Readers' comments:

# Section 2  Planning and Preparation

## Whose task is it, anyway?

The range of people who may get involved in planning, preparing and running training events has dramatically increased in the last twenty years. The scale of events also vary quite considerably, from ad hoc, informal sessions for teams within organisations, through 'whole organisation' training up to national conferences. These conferences frequently offer state-of-the-art presentations on anything from bullying, care in the community, through to the NVQ revolution, and the perennial, where are we going? I was a presenter at one of these mega-events a couple of years ago in a massive conference hotel some miles outside of Dublin. I'd been presenting workshops (with my Scottish colleague Howie Armstrong) for youth and community workers across the whole of Ireland on the use of games and group work techniques. At the end of each day in the main hall, bits of our presentations which had been filmed were broadcast in multi-media splendour onto gigantic split screens towering behind the plenary presenters. That and a special filmed performance of Bono and U2 as well!

The factors that have led to this greater involvement in organising training are quite a mixed bag. They are even conflictual. On one hand there has been the development of a do-it-yourself ethos, on the other, a move towards training being a modular, highly structured set of experiences which are certified, accredited and supposedly homogeneous and only carried out by similarly accredited trainers. Whilst I would hope that there is much in this book that may be helpful for the latter group, this book is primarily aimed at helping a wider range of people involved in people-services to get involved in meeting their own training needs.

For some of the professions concerned there has been a desire for less 'professionalised' training, coupled with cut-backs in training budgets and an increasing belief that people need to take responsibility for their own training and career development. This change means that in some contexts more training is organised on a 'bottom-up' basis of being related directly to the needs and views of the participants. This has served to de-mystify 'training'. No longer is it seen automatically as necessary to engage 'trainers' and 'training officers' to fulfil all the organisational and planning tasks. Similarly, the shift of emphasis has encouraged more individuals who are employed as professional training organisers to:

- Canvass the opinions of the likely participants.
- Look for styles and methods of presentation that are collaborative, and are appropriate both culturally and in subject.
- Use the skills and knowledge of practitioners in the planning process.

The most effective way to approach the task is to look carefully at the points in Checklist 2.1 (see page 32), which can help to determine and define what is possible.

Looking at the particular 'answers' you arrive at from consideration of Checklist 2.1 should assist in the structuring of the best possible planning and preparation team. Essentially this is a process for quickly assessing the likely tasks and matching these with an organisational structure which can handle the volume of the work, be seen as acceptable and competent to all 'the players' in Checklist 2.1, and importantly be **able to work together**!

# Horses for courses

This old saying is singularly appropriate for the organisers of training. I was asked to produce an in-house daily conference newsletter at one national housing conference on tenant participation, together with the post-conference report. Funding had been obtained to subsidise the event through government sources, and those attending were a broadly representative cross-section of policy-makers and councillors, housing professionals and tenants. The organisers decided that the event should be used as a political campaigning platform, and the opening speaker, who was also the government's party chairman, was promptly reduced to red-faced apoplexy by being introduced by the conference chair:

*'And I'd like to welcome … an ex-MP!'*

This proved predictably amusing to many of the participants, dramatic and ironic, but politically and financially naive, and, in retrospect, the organisers had to admit that it proved an expensive piece of abuse, as subsequent funding became harder to obtain. 'Campaigning' and 'training' can prove to be uncomfortable bedfellows! The real lesson is one which should concern all training organisers:

*How can training best achieve our aims?*

In Section 1 of this book, there are a number of checklists designed to help training organisers arrive at a set of aims. Most of the material in Section 2 is geared to maximising the opportunities for trainers to organise themselves more effectively in order to achieve their stated aims. A first stage will be in deciding:

*What is required from the organisational team?*

Having considered the main options for the event and the players, the tasks that need to be performed may become clearer. This should help organisers to determine their needs in terms of the composition and size of the planning and organising group. In commerce, the organisation of training and conference-type events is often bought *en bloc* from outside consultancies and specialist organisations. This is one of the options for people-work agencies, though in most instances, the benefits of getting rid of the workload and having a professional team who undertakes the work are outweighed by the negatives. These may include significant loss of control over content and methods; lack of professional understanding on central concerns and issues; and, very importantly, the potential alienation of participants, who, in the social care and education fields, like to act as partners in the planning, preparation and implementation stages.

# Organising group tasks

There can even be occasions where **the process** of organising training and involvement in the event can be as important as outcomes. Checklist 2.2 (see pag 33) shows some group tasks.

A small in-house event will require only a fraction of these tasks to be undertaken, consequently needing a much less complex servicing group. A substantial, residential conference for 100 plus participants needs the whole list to be considered, even if some of the areas are deemed inappropriate. The planning group must:

- Allocate and delegate the tasks in the list.
- Draw up a schedule for the event, with dates when action is required by.
- In most groups, it is best to have some sort of defined job titles, and have them minuted, so that everyone can be kept to task.

(An example of a typical task list is given at the beginning of Section 3 on page 51.)

This naturally leads to a further set of planning questions in Checklist 2.3 (see page 34).

No answers to the above questions are 'right' or 'wrong', but from experience, they are,

- a) frequently overlooked, or left until too late in the planning and preparation process,
- b) some of the fundamental concerns which can make or break a people-work training event.

# The audience

In establishing aims for any particular piece of training, the nature of the audience should be paramount in the minds of organisers. In most cases, the organising group will be representative of at least a significant sector of the intended audience or at least have very real understanding of the work and job roles of the likely participants. Where this is not possible, for instance, when social workers are trying to put on an event for magistrates, there needs to be especial attention paid to briefing both the organisers and the proposed training staff on the exact constituency of the participants. As these may come from a very wide background, in the case of events on subjects like criminal justice (police; probation; law; social work; courts; offenders' groups; reparation schemes, etc.) extra preparation, 'homework', if you like, must be done by the organisers. This can be accomplished by soliciting views, comments, information on needs, through:

- Direct contact with individuals from the potential audience groupings.
- Use of questionnaires or survey forms sent to a cross-section of organisations or to all applicants for places.

By these methods it is possible to shape the event in a way which matches it to the expectations of participants, and makes the planning of the individual components of the event in workshops and smaller units much more responsive to individual experience levels and individual needs. Which 'hook' is used to attract an audience depends very much on the individual piece of training or event. Self-interest plays a big part in most people's motivation for 'betterment', 'self-improvement' or 'career development'. In the people-services, training events may be organised to:

- Improve the delivery of services.
- Improve working relations in staff teams.
- Communicate information.
- Understand new legislation and working practices and their implications for different practitioner groups.

- Develop practice and management skills.
- Reach measurable standards of performance.
- Improve staff motivation and teamworking.
- Discuss reaction to 'change', and possibly inappropriately offer 'rewards' to staff members for compliance.

Participants at many training events arrive not only with pens and a notepad but with a shopping bag full of expectations, fears, and work and personal problems. No training organisers can be expected to anticipate, and meet, all the needs generated through this assortment of hopes and fears. What can be predicted is that some worries are common to all trainees and students. Inevitably, participants may be worried about:

- The 'power' of the trainer.
- The expectations of their employers that they get skilled or trained.
- Failing to get the approved certificate or accreditation.
- The possibility that they may be out of their depth, de-skilled or belittled by the training process.
- The fear of the 'unknown'.
- Being vulnerable in front of colleagues or peers.

To overcome some of these resistances to training, the organisers should try to find out as much as possible about the '*potential*', and at a later stage, the '*actual*' audience or participants. The sort of checklist you may wish to modify is presented in Checklist 2.4 (see page 35).

There is a considerable difference in the style of programme which would be appropriate for a group of hearing-impaired children from an inner city housing estate; a group of directors of education; an inter-disciplinary group of psychologists, psychiatrists, teachers, health workers, social workers and doctors looking at disclosure in child sexual abuse cases. And so, the 'horses for courses' principle holds good. Getting the structure and style of an event right for the intended audience will greatly influence the level of success of the venture, and, if the programme 'looks wrong', you may not even get any punters to attend! There is an old proverb, often attributed to Confucius, which is pertinent:

**If the language is not correct, then what is said is not what is meant. If what is said is not what is meant, then what ought to be done remains undone.**

In preparing for training events, it is not always possible to obtain all the information organisers might like about the nature and the background of the audience. Some of these problems can be overcome at the actual event by asking participants to **self-select** preferred workshops, lectures and seminars based on their own preferences, interests, knowledge and experience. A small, homogeneous group, meeting to discuss a subject which all the participants know well, can have a more intimate and experiential structure of sharing, compared to a large conference, where most participants are considering the subject for perhaps the first time. In this second instance, the nature of the audience knowledge base will pre-determine a higher level of information-giving. The type of audience also needs to be considered in relation to:

- accessibility to venues

- linguistic and literacy levels

- any relevant issues relating to gender, race or special needs

- confidentiality

- the organisational structures in which they work

Community-based training often needs to be handled locally and in teams. Specialist and multi-disciplinary training may take place more effectively in central locations; workplace training will usually involve assessment of practice, plus some information-sharing and tutorials; whole organisation training may work best where staff at different levels of seniority and with different jobs are either split up, or remain organised in their working units. It is perfectly possible for participants and trainers or consultants to agree 'contracts' for training. In this case, the expectations, process and programme can all be clarified in advance and help make training a truly participative exercise.

> **The key is for organisers to consider carefully the implications of training options, so as to meet the needs of the greatest number of participants.**

## Finding a suitable training venue

The chicken and egg problem of: *plan an event first and sell it, or test interest and then plan an event*, often surfaces when organising training events. It may not pose a problem when you are organising in-service training where you know that you will be using the local authority training centre, and when you know exactly how many staff should be attending an event. However, this certainty rarely exists in other forms of training event. For the organisers, it can cause quite a headache, and it has a knock-on effect for those working in the conference venue industry, who can sometimes, and justly, be critical of sloppy organisation from the people-services sector.

The best that the organiser or organising committee can do is to try and work out a checklist of what the ideal scenario would look like, and then create some fall-back situations to cope with potential disasters. To arrive at the best checklist for finding the most suitable venue, the organisers must already have some idea of the type of programme, but not necessarily the detail, and a guesstimate for the maximum, and possibly the optimum number of participants. Based on the experience of a number of organising committees I have worked with, the Checklist 2.5 (see page 36) may prove useful, possibly with some degree of adaptation to meet varying or special needs.

Some of the details should be possible for the organisers to agree on as 'aims' or at least 'benchmarks' at the planning stage, for example:

> *We would like not to charge more than £X per head for a three-day residential conference, sited somewhere in the north-east of England, for about 120-150 participants, with about 100 needing accommodation.*

This sort of early agreement on 'intent' can enable the first stages of negotiation to take place with possible venues, checking availability and facilities. I would suggest using a copy of Checklist 2.5 for each venue, so that there is an easy comparison available for the organisers as they short-list the best options and narrow down the choice. I'd suggest looking at facilities first and then moving on to considering costings.

Checklist 2.5 is fairly detailed and is based on experience in organising events in the people-services. It might not fit the differently motivated world of business conventions or corporate events, or high-key international events such as the annual UK Housing Conference (usually at Harrogate) where the key questions are more about the exhibition services, levels of hospitality, and very particular forms of back-up service.

However, it should provide the basis for gaining a fair amount of information from any venue or location visit. These can be time consuming and may be costly in terms of travel, but any larger event needs proper researching. Usually, the event organisers will nominate at least two of their number to visit potential venues and check out the facilities. This decision can be a very expensive one and should be given careful consideration. A couple of points also worth considering are:

- Should you visit the venue incognito?
- Can you check out with previous users what they thought about the venue?

Visits to venues can actually be fun and your organising committee may gain a few nice meals at the venues' expense! Either way, they are a necessity, and might as well be enjoyed.

## Potential venue problems

One suspects that a whole book might be written just on this subject. Planning and preparation, if carried out thoroughly, does help to overcome a lot of the potential hazards, but there is always the unforeseen, and thinking about *what might happen if ...* can be worthwhile. A number of the points in Checklist 2.6 have already been listed in the venues Checklist 2.5, but some will come to light only when the organisers are at the point of signing contractual agreements. Again, it's not a definitive list, but it should identify some of the potential pitfalls.

## How to choose a venue

People-work covers an enormous range of communities, professionals and voluntary groups. The issues which are raised make the planning and organisation of events very different from many similar corporate events for industry and commerce. For instance, a participative event held for 200 partially sighted participants in a Butlin's camp out of season, is very different from a high-powered sales conference to motivate sales executives in the publishing industry.

**The choice of a venue will depend a lot on the level of finance available and the nature of the audience. Other major factors include accessibility, style and the duration of the proposed event. Keep these in mind when you or the organising group are considering options for venues.**

The locations and types of venues where training events could take place is almost limitless. Imagination and flexibility can create the ideal 'off the wall' situation in which creative training can take place. I have personally organised events billed as 'training' for social care staff in remote island bothies; on a twenty-tonne, 68-foot narrow boat; in a scout camp; under canvas in Snowdonia, and at a holiday camp; so try to avoid being hidebound by the convention that training automatically means hotels, conference suites or colleges and universities.

Also, there has been a significant growth in numbers of independent and private full-time trainers, consultants and organisations who now offer services to statutory and voluntary agencies across the range of social services and education. These people represent a 'resource' of experience. Managers of venues who really understand what the aim of a training event is, and how their facilities can be utilised to the maximum effect, can also offer a high level of expertise and advice. Someone from these two groups may be able to organise not only programmes of bespoke training, but also search for appropriate venues as part of their services. Checklist 2.7 (see page 40) lists some possible locations for venues.

There are a variety of publishers and venue finders who publish guides and who provide useful listings of potential venues which would be suitable for conferences and the larger-scale people-services training events. Professional venue finders exist who act as brokers operating between clients and the venue. They usually offer their services free to the client and get their commission from the venue. An extensive list of venue finders is to be found in the annual *Corporate Event Services Guide* (see below). Useful sources for information and listings include:

*Corporate Event Services Guide*, Corporate Event Publishing Ltd., 38c The Broadway, Crouch End, London N8 9SU. 020 8348 2332. www.cesbook.co.uk

*British Association of Conference Destinations*, 6th Floor, Charles House, 148-149 Great Charles St, Birmingham, West Midlands B3 3HT. 0121 212 1400. www.bacd.org.uk

*Conference Blue Green Book*, CMP Data and Information Services, Riverbank House, Angel Lane, Tonbridge, Kent TN9 1SE. 01732 367301. www.venuefinder.com

*Historic Houses and Gardens Directory*, Hudsons, High Wardington House, Upper Wardington, Oxfordshire OX17 1SP. 01295 750750. www.hudsons.co.uk

I've heard of the following two professional bodies of conference organisers, though I have not used them personally:

*Association of British Professional Conference Organisers* (ABPCO), 6th Floor, Charles House, 148-149 Great Charles St, Birmingham, West Midlands B3 3HT. 0121 212 4141

*Association for Conferences and Events* (ACE), Riverside House, High Street, Huntingdon, Cambridgeshire PE29 3SG. 01480 457595

And information on venues may also be obtained from:

*Venuemasters*, The Workstation, Paternoster Row, Sheffield S1 2BX. 0114 249 3090. www.venuemasters.co.uk

*British Association of Conference Towns*, 1st Floor, Elizabeth House, 22 Suffolk Street Birmingham B1 1LS. 021 616 1400

*British Tourist Authority* and *Visit Britain*, Thames Tower, Black's Road, London W6 9EL. 020 8846 9000. www.britishtouristauthority.org

*British University Accommodation Consortium Ltd*, Box Number 817, University Park, Nottingham NG7 2RD. 0115 950 4571 (linked to Venuemasters above)

A search through the local Yellow Pages and Thomson directories for geographical areas you are interested in can produce some additional options. My local listings, for instance, offered up a local wildlife park and the warden's centre at a National Trust park in the Jurassic Coast Park – not venues I would have thought of. Many companies and local authorities have their own training venues and some are under-utilised. Depending upon your needs, it may be possible to negotiate access and special deals with organisations as disparate as the local police force, British Telecom or even a publishing company.

One additional aspect should be considered. Is the event a one-off, or part of a continuing, on-going process of training and education? If it is the latter, you may be able to get a reduced rate from a venue, if you agree to a 'package' price for the current event and future training, even if the dates for the rest of the programme are somewhat uncertain. Venues are in business to make money, and it is a highly competitive business where 'deals' can be accommodated. Do make sure that any deal is confirmed in writing from a person with authority to make such arrangements.

## Publicity and marketing

The social services and education sectors have taken a while to catch up with their colleagues in health and housing as far as running profitable and very high profile conferences is concerned. That, however, is not the major concern of this book. The contention here is that training events come in all shapes and sizes, and that it is just as important therefore to improve the 'image' of community-type training events and inter-professional training. This is especially true when welfare services often take a hammering in the media. Instead, trainers need to stress factors such as: empowerment, partnership working, stakeholding, networking and the effective provision of services such as community care.

Failure to 'sell' events effectively has often been the downfall of some of the most professional and carefully programmed events. Marshall McLuhan coined the phrase: 'The medium is the message'. And that medium and message need to be presented powerfully in ways which will attract participants. Marketing in the people-services is 90 per cent about knowing the audience and utilising this knowledge through well-presented publicity material, which:

- Is worded appropriately for the intended audience.
- Conveys all the necessary information, simply and effectively.
- Is presented in a style and quality appropriate for the audience.
- Is distributed in ways which will access the intended audiences.

Staff who make the decision to work in the people-services are usually motivated towards caring for others, working with the disadvantaged, and trying to change society and communities in ways beneficial to the majority. The skills and attitudes prevalent in these staff are not particularly conducive to hard-line selling and the market economy approach of the 2000s, though the growth of a substantial private (and not-for-profit) training and consultancy sector has created a changed attitude towards the profit motive. The outcome, in many cases, is that training has still kept true to a caring spirit, is generally priced according to need rather than market forces, and is often subsidised based on the desirability of creating better skilled staff and improved service delivery.

This 'feels' right within the social welfare sector, and runs counter to some of the more negative aspects of the Thatcherite legacy of materialism, market economies and competition. But trainers have learned some useful and positive lessons from the changing culture inherited from the 1980s and 1990s. The local financial management of schools, the spread of home-ownership through the Right to Buy, competitive tendering and budget holding are all now parts of this new world.

As a consequence, marketing is no longer an alien concept to welfare agencies. The need to be 'proactive' in selling services, including training services, has become much more widely accepted. In many cases, voluntary agencies and some statutory agencies, universities and colleges and the private sector are all competing for the 'training market' in the 'people-services'. In pragmatic terms, this makes the effective use of publicity even more critical if agencies are reliant for part of their income on the 'take-up' of training places.

More is said later in this section (see *Programming*, page 29) on considerations for getting the programme content right, but marketing inevitably depends upon having a good 'product' to sell. It is also important for trainers to be aware of what competition they are running against, both in terms of clashing dates and similar themes and subjects. In the people-services, there is usually a limited amount of funding available for training and conference participation, and organisers will be 'competing' for their share.

Training event leaflets and publicity can also serve a two-way function. They may be the main vehicle for asking questions of the participants, which will help the organisers to obtain necessary administrative information on everything from accommodation and workshop choices, special needs and requirements of participants, through to training expectations. This allows organisers to be flexible and to modify aspects of the programme as a response. (It may be worth referring back to the section on *The Audience* for more ideas on the sort of information that may help tailor the event to the intended participants.) This information, if gathered in a way that fits the requirements of a previously constructed computer database program, can help to simplify and speed up the registration procedure. Checklist 2.8 (see page 41) shows what might be included in the publicity material. Once again, you could use it as a form to fill in your own specific 'answers' and requirements.

## Publicity material design and layout

In these days of desk top publishing being available at very least through a word processing package like Word, it is relatively easy for many agencies to produce their own training publicity up to quite a high standard. Photos and graphics can be included, but the trick is to not to get too carried away with the image, thereby forgetting the content. When the publicity material is produced, it is important that someone with an artistic or design eye makes sure that it is attractive and appropriate for the audience and professionally correct, unambiguous, and does not contain any sexist or racist phrases or undertones. Leaflets do not need to cost a vast amount of money to promote training events effectively. Figures 2.2 and 2.3 (see pages 49 and 50) show some examples.

The size of the brochure will depend upon the amount of information to be included. The most popular size is an A4 sheet of paper folded down to A5. Sometimes, booking leaflets use two folds rather than one, which is a form of gatefold. This format can provide a useful compromise in giving two panels of information which is retained by the applicant, and one panel for returning to the organisers with application and registration details. A lot depends on whether you are going to print two or three hundred leaflets in-house, or are going to hand the material for the leaflet on a disk or CD Rom over to a design firm or printers for a larger scale production.

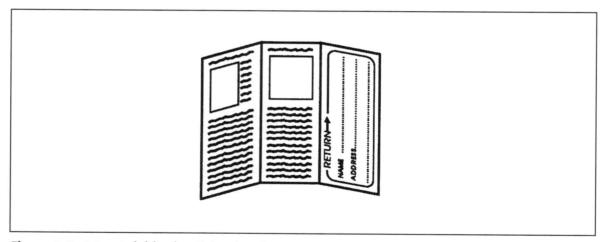

Figure 2.1: A4 gatefold advertising brochure

## Publicity material distribution

A good leaflet or programme is of little or no use if it is produced too late to attract an audience, or if it fails to reach the intended audience. So, as an organiser of training, make sure that someone has this task in hand and that the publicity is adequate to create the sort of take-up response needed to make the event viable. In direct-mail marketing, the effectiveness of a mail shot of any kind depends upon how carefully targeted the lists used are. Good publicity, coupled sometimes with incentives such as accreditation or 'certificates of competence', or a free book or report given as part of the training package, can increase the level of applications. As a rule of thumb, a ten per cent response rate to any leaflet is considered very good. See Checklist 2.9 (see page 43) for ways to market training.

# Programming

No, this isn't an introductory course for computer programmers!

The **programme** in any training event or conference must be thought through as carefully as possible. At the earliest possible time, the planning group should be ready to commit themselves publicly to the programme in a brochure, advert or other publicity leaflet. The sorts of things to bear in mind are set out in Checklist 2.10 (see page 44).

# Communication with speakers, session and workshop leaders

A conference, a one-off half-day training event, and an accredited training course will each involve potential problems, mostly to do with communication. Problems may arise through poor liaison between the planners/organisers and the session facilitators/leaders. The sort of areas which need to be clarified as far as possible are listed in Checklist 2.11 (see page 46).

From the point of view of the speakers and the session facilitators, they will have their own list of concerns and 'wants'. The later parts of this book on **styles and methods** of presentation may be of interest and use to some of them. Many of the likely concerns will be practical and pragmatic, for instance:

- Can the session meet the established aims?
- Is it feasible in the context of the place, people and time slot?
- Is it likely to be appropriate for the participants and meet their expectations and needs?
- Will the necessary information about the event, and equipment and materials needed be available to run the session?

Checklists 2.1 – 2.11 give a pretty fair picture of the sorts of areas which need detailed planning and preparation. Essentially, speakers and facilitators should feel that they are partners in the event and that they have been *consulted* in all relevant aspects, without actually burdening them with the administration of the event.

Practical aspects concerning the nature of the rooms to be used, such as whether they have adequate tables and chairs, power sockets, cables, lighting, etc. can easily get overlooked and can ruin an otherwise well-prepared session. Likewise, if the programme schedule is tight and participants become lost in transit between sessions, as they were in a couple of university sites I've used in the past, there is a tendency for participants to take the easy option and disappear off over the horizon! Other potential hazards which I have encountered include:

- Organisers who intervene or interfere with sessions in progress, thus inhibiting participants and throwing facilitators and speakers 'off-balance'.
- Facilitators who know their subject, but do not wish to enable participants, instead preferring to show-off their knowledge and skills.
- Participants who have been 'sent' to events and are a disruptive influence.

- Ill-prepared facilitators who haven't done their preparation, can't run sessions, or who are perhaps deputising for absent colleagues.
- Sessions where the presentation doesn't fit the 'billing', and is obviously geared to another audience and another subject.

It may also be worth giving speakers and session leaders a short checklist form covering their material needs. For an example which I have used see Checklist 2.12 (see page 47).

## Exhibitions and market places

Conference organisers can boost their income levels, and at the same time add another dimension to their event by putting on some sort of market place or exhibition. In the people-services many organisations are both using and providing services and facilities. It is quite usual for social work agencies to have books and reports for sale, residential facilities for hire, training services and courses on offer, and a host of other available products such as videos, equipment for special needs groups, training games, etc. Therefore it is in their own interests for training organisers to seriously consider whether their particular event lends itself to providing space for displaying other agencies' wares.

If you expect agencies to pay for space in a market place or exhibition, it is important to provide the proper back-up. This will usually mean providing:

- Tables and chairs for exhibitors.
- Power supply and possibly lighting.
- Possibly display stands.
- Some sort of food and hospitality facilities.
- A leaflet or short handout giving details of the event and the market place exhibition facilities, including a layout design of the spaces to be used and stand sizes. (Potential exhibitors will want to know how many participants are expected; who they are and how much time they will have in which to display their wares.)

More elaborate demands would include requests for display stand preparation, flowers and decorations, staging, a bar facility and photographic or video equipment.

Book publishers, bookstall services, equipment suppliers, related service industries, public services such as the police, fire and ambulance services, local firms operating in the geographical vicinity of the venue, indeed anyone who might wish to target your training event participants, could be your customer and potential contributor to your exhibition area, market place and financial income!

## Entertainment

The organisation of the entertainment for any long training event can take a little care and attention to find the most appropriate form of leisure amusement for your participants. Usually it is best to leave the organisation of entertainment to members of the organising group who enjoy this type of task, have some contacts, and enjoy a little 'wheeling and dealing', which is all part of the entertainment business!

Options which I have used include:

- rock, blues, jazz and folk groups
- theatre productions
- cabaret and alternative cabaret
- mime and circus performers
- discos
- karaoke
- sketches and cabarets produced by the participants
- film shows
- sports activities

Obviously it is important to have the entertainment on at appropriate times in the overall programme, and at times which are likely to fit the mood of the participants. It may also be necessary to offer options if the age range and interests of the participants vary quite a lot. Some may prefer snooker or pool competition or a badminton or squash tournament, or even a round of golf, so try to think laterally, and offer a range of choices.

The staff at the venue are often a good source for local entertainers, but make sure that you see or hear the performers, or at least a tape or CD, before booking them. The venue may also be able to arrange for the provision of lighting and sound gear and any special needs. Often it is best to use performers whom you know will turn up and who are likely to go down well with your particular audience. When booking performers, Checklist 2.13 (see page 48) may help you in your negotiations.

During the event:

- Ensure that the entertainers have someone to liaise with and that they can get whatever assistance and help they require.
- Check out with the venue over any noise problems, potential hassles with other venue users, neighbours, etc.
- Organise payments and other benefits for entertainers, as per agreements.

## Checklist 2.1: Planning and preparation options

What are the implications for the organisational structure of:

- The subject and theme of the training?
- The type of audience?
- The size and length of the event?
- The style(s) and methods of presentation likely to be used?
- Budget restrictions/availability?

There are a number of potential sets of 'players' in training. It is well worthwhile considering, in each instance, which groups need to be consulted, or at least kept in mind, for the particular event you are proposing to run. These 'players' could include:

- Those paying for the training.
- Those who employ potential participants.
- Any organisation or agency sponsoring an event.
- Policy-makers and local and national politicians.
- The planning group.
- Administrative staff.
- Speakers, facilitators, workshop organisers.
- Media representatives.
- Venue management and staff.
- Participants.

**Try using this list as the basis for an exercise on who is potentially involved in your training event?**

# Checklist 2.2: Organising group tasks

These can include:

- Acting as a think-tank and generating programme, subject and personnel ideas.
- Setting the style.
- Setting aims and ensuring that they are met.
- Organising the selection and booking of a venue.
- Liaising with speakers and workshop leaders.
- Financing the event, dealing with sponsors.
- Marketing and publicity.
- Dealing with the media and specialist press.
- Administration before the event for bookings, accommodation, special requirements.
- Preparation of pre-event participants' 'packs'.
- Registration and administration at the event problem-chasing at the event.
- Transport arrangements.
- Entertainment.
- Reports, newsletters and other follow-up.
- Evaluation and monitoring of the event.

# Checklist 2.3: Planning questions

■ Do the event organisers need to use the event as a platform for their ideas or views? Or, for those of a host organisation?

■ Is it appropriate for organisers to take on 'active' roles as chairpersons, speakers and workshop leaders during the event?

■ Are there any pragmatic or political reasons for inviting the participation of certain individuals or representatives from particular organisations on the organising group?

■ Is it a good idea to have one person in an overall, co-ordinating capacity for the event organisation?

■ Is it worth considering 'buying-in' some elements of support, possibly for administration, from outside of the group?

■ Has active consultation taken place with all the interested and influential parties for the event?

## Checklist 2.4: Audience or participant

Age .................     Sex .........................     Job title ...............................................................

Organisation...........................................     Geographical area worked in.......................................

Main qualifications/interests:

What does your current job entail?

What experience do you have on the training subject?

What do you hope to get out of the training session?

Do you have any concerns about attending?

Any special needs regarding diet, health, child care etc.?

# Checklist 2.5: Venues

The initial factors to consider are:

**Name of venue:**                                       Contact person:

Address:                                                tel:

                                                        fax:

                                                        e-mail:

**Location:**

Travel to and from:

*(potential for special deals)*

Train:

Air:

Car:                                                    Car parking:

Bus and tube:

Time of year/duration:

Availability of venue dates:

Comments on access, location and other aspects:

**Facilities**

**Residential accommodation:**

  En suite/not en suite:

  Number of single:

  Number of double:

  Number of family:

  Dormitories:

  Other *(describe)*:

  Comment on quality:

  Availability of higher grade rooms for guest speakers:

**Plenary rooms:**

  Number of rooms and maximum capacities:
  *(Check on layout and flexibility of seating)*

  Notes on audio-visual, computer and other facilities:
  *(For instance, check microphones and speakers through the PA)*
  *(Ask about projection/video/OHP and tape slide facilities)*
  *(Check on noise problems/ventilation/heating/smoking rules)*

  Comments:

→

**Checklist 2.5 contd…**

**Workshop/seminar rooms:**
*(Check on layout and seating flexibility)*

Number of rooms and maximum capacities:

Notes on audio-visual and other facilities:
*(Check mics and speakers through the PA, availability of flip charts/OHPs)*

Comments:

**Layout general:**
*(Are there any problems to do with the size and design of the venue? Access problems for disabled? Split levels, too far between rooms to walk, cold and draughty areas, etc.)*
*(Is it OK for organisers to move furniture about in workshop and plenary rooms?)*

**Exhibition space:**
*(Is there any suitable space available? Any restrictions on use/duration? Are display stands and lighting available?)*

**Registration and reception arrangements:**

Comments:

**Catering:**

Menu options:

Catering styles:
*(Self-catering/self-service/table service/buffet/outside caterers, etc.)*

Vegetarian/vegan and special menus:

Facilities for special 'high table' functions:

Facilities for coffees and teas during work breaks:

Comments:
*(Quality, speed of service, presentation, cleanliness, flexibility, formal or informal)*

Bar and times *(if required)*:

**Social areas:**
*(TV room/games room/snooker/pool, etc.)*

→

**Checklist 2.5 contd…**

**Possibilities for entertainment:**

Theatre/dance/film show/disco capabilities:

Staging/PA facilities/lighting rig/video or film projection equipment:

**Special facilities:**
*(For instance, crèche and baby-sitting service, disabled access to various facilities, toilets, photocopying, computer and Internet access, printing facilities, telephones and fax, separate administration area/room for the organisers, sports hall, swimming pool, gymnasium, security arrangements.)*

**Local amenities/tourist attractions:**
*(Any special deals?)*

**Audio-visual support:**
*(Is there a competent electrician/technician on site?)*

**Other organisations who have used the venue:**
*(Contact name(s), telephone number and address)*

**Attitude:**

General:

Are the staff attitudes appropriate for the audience?

Do they seem competent/friendly?

Were there any overt or covert signs of racist or sexist attitudes? Sexist or offensive pictures or calendars?

**Any other requirements?**

**Costing:**

Rates per participant per day including agreed meals:

Rates per participant including accommodation:

Extras:
*(Coffees/teas/equipment hire/entertainment etc.)*

Will the event be the only one going on? If there are others, what are the potential areas of difficulty, such as cultural differences, noise, over-burdening the catering?

Date ......................................... Who visited ...................................................................................

# Checklist 2.6: Potential problems

■ Insurance cover is getting prohibitively expensive, but may still be worth considering against: event cancellation; injury or death of participants; theft and damage of equipment and participants' belongings; and assault. Check with the venue regarding what cover they already have, or can extend, to cover your event.

■ Noise, complaints from the venue management and/or other users.

■ Noise caused by building work, noisy equipment (especially heating and ventilation systems).

■ Non-appearance of speakers or workshop leaders.

■ Problems with adverse weather.

■ Strikes and transport problems.

■ Problems caused by damage to the venue.

■ Clashes of culture with the venue management.

■ Competing events.

■ Poor marketing or publicity material.

■ Insufficient attention to budgeting and costing.

■ Administrative problems caused through not confirming arrangements in advance and in writing.

■ Slow catering arrangements which cause programming problems.

## Checklist 2.7: Possible venues

- Hotels

- Specialist conference halls or centres

- Universities and colleges

- Residential centres

- Cinemas and theatres

- Community facilities: centres, halls, schools

- Holiday camps

- Centres and other buildings owned by voluntary organisations

- Camping sites

- Outward bound and similar facilities

- Overseas locations

- Boats and ships of various kinds

# Checklist 2.8: Publicity material

Event title ..........................................................................................................................
*(Is it part of a series or course?)*

Sub-title ..............................................................................................................................

Organisers/sponsors ........................................................................................................

Venue ..................................................................................................................................

Location ..............................................................................................................................

Date(s) and start time ....................................................................................................

Aim(s) ..................................................................................................................................

............................................................................................................................................

Who is it intended for? ...................................................................................................

An indication of the level, or levels of content (if applicable):




Programme:






*(Try to give as much detail as possible on input titles/subjects; speakers and their background; workshop and seminar options; teaching styles and methods; other 'selling points' like awarding of certificates/accreditation; special features – videos, facilities for handicapped, crèche facilities, reductions for unemployed, relevance to the workplace, exhibitions.* **Remember: stress the benefits of the training, not just the features***. If the timetable is available at the time of producing the publicity material, include it. Consider including comments from previous participants, where appropriate.)* **(Note:** *Use tick boxes for responses and choices of options. These might include preference boxes for vegetarian/kosher/vegan food.)*


Costs/charges ....................................................................................................................
*(Include options, if applicable, for day and residential rates; couples; members of specific organisations; children; special requirements; unemployed.)*



Closing date for applications ........................................................................................

→

**Checklist 2.8 contd…**

Payment details .........................................................................................................................
*(Include who cheques should be made out to; any invoicing and deposit arrangements; whether VAT is payable or not; cancellation conditions and refund arrangements; contact name and address and a telephone number/fax for contact enquiries.)*

Participant details:

Name of person submitting the form .........................................................................................

Position .................................................................................................................................

Organisation .........................................................................................................................

Address .................................................................................................................................

Telephone ..................................................... E-mail ..........................................................

*(Note: It is probably worth putting in a 'disclaimer' regarding the programme being 'correct at the time of going to press, but the organisers cannot guarantee the appearance of all speakers, or first choice of workshops, and they retain the right to change the programme and price as necessary'. Remember that a booking form constitutes a legal contract.)*

# Checklist 2.9: Marketing the event

The main ways to market training are through:

- Direct mail shots to named individuals and organisations.

- Editorial copy, inserts or adverts placed in specialist and professional magazines and journals.

- Personal contact – word of mouth – bush telegraph telephone follow-up/information (targeted at specific people, if possible).

- Inter-agency and inter-professional links.

- Publicity at other courses, training events and exhibitions.

- Purchasing lists of names or printed labels from brokers and directory publishers.

- The media, through TV, national and local radio and newspapers may also be a channel for recruiting participants to some courses and events.

# Checklist 2.10: Programming

### Styles of presentation

What is the expected balance between *large group* plenaries, lectures, speeches, panel discussions; smaller group workshops, seminars, buzz groups, special interest groups, professional groups, team/geographical groups, inter/multi-agency groups; reading/thinking time; social and entertainment time; eating/drinking time?

### Who is doing the presenting/facilitating?

It may be important to have some well-known, controversial or respected 'front' names to attract an audience. You may also need to balance the speakers/workshop leaders according to a mixture of practitioners and planners, or, academics and managers, or, politicians and funders. Planning groups also need to think about the balance of 'presenters' in terms of their age, backgrounds, sex, cultural and ethnic backgrounds.

### Time, duration and place

What are the consequences, for instance, in putting on your 'best' presentation first thing on a three-day programme? Will the participants respond better to a presentation if there is an advance handout in the conference pack? Some rooms may suit different types of presentation better than others. A 'dirty', active workshop needs an appropriate space which will not lead to the venue manager climbing the walls in annoyance at blu-tack on those very same walls.

### Balance

It is worth remembering that all participants can get bored, even if they are very interested in a subject. Try to ensure that 'involvement' is kept to a maximum level, where appropriate for the subject. If a subject or skill area has a range of options/opinions associated with it, think about how the varying points of view can be presented to achieve balance and debate.

### Group composition

For some workshops and presentations it may be best to try and arrange for particular participants to be in particular groups. This could be because the aim is to 'unblock' a team, or to make sure that different professionals are becoming accustomed to working together. It is also very likely that workshop leaders and facilitators will have their own preferences for how many participants will work best in their group setting.

### Levels of presentation

In a lot of training events, the level of experience of participants, their previous training, and the intended level of the information to be offered will each be critical to the success or otherwise of the session. Each individual component of the programme may need to be considered in its own right. Teaching about computer skills, or the working of the Children Act, each requires a different approach. And also, some presenters will feel more comfortable with particular styles of presentation.

→

**Checklist 2.10 contd...**

**Publicity material**
Make sure that all the relevant programme information is described accurately and as fully as necessary in the publicity material. If participants need to make choices about which workshops or other sessions they will attend, this needs to be agreed in advance.

**Language**
A good programme dressed up in incomprehensible jargon will not be appreciated. The publicity material and any conference pack material and handouts need to be put through a 'plain English' test, and also checked for 'isms' of the sexist and racist type.

**Equipment/materials**
For many workshops and plenary sessions, equipment and materials need preparing in advance. Some items, such as computers, specialist video film, or a theatre group may need to be booked considerably in advance. The responsibility for these tasks may rest with the event organiser or the individual session leaders. There is also likely to be liaison needed with the venue managers and technical staff, where their 'hardware' such as computers, video machines and overhead projection equipment is going to be used.

**Breaks and intervals**
In any programme, the intermissions, coffee and tea breaks, etc. may be as important as some of the inputs. This is for two reasons. First, the participants need to get their collective breath back, have time for a bit of reflection, and secondly, have a chance for informal discussion and debate on issues raised. Make sure that the breaks are long enough and come frequently enough in the programme to facilitate this sort of process.

**Evaluation and feedback**
Have these been thought about? What methods/means are the organisers going to use to obtain feedback from participants during and after the event? Can the effectiveness of the training/inputs be monitored? Is it possible to evaluate the effect of the training on subsequent practice?

**Organisational roles**
Are these clearly defined and allocated amongst the organisers and any others co-opted into the planning network?

**Finally, ask yourself 'does the programme look as though it will meet the needs of the participants and intended aims of organisers?'**

---

# Checklist 2.11: Communication with session leaders, speakers and workshop leaders

- Have fees and any other 'extras' such as travel costs, administrative costs, subsistence and accommodation costs been agreed?

- Are the expectations of what the aims of the event; the aims of the organisers, and the aims of the facilitators all in accord?

- Are the organisers in a position to provide the facilitators with a 'briefing note' of any kind?

- Are the speakers or session leaders expected to provide advance material for the event 'pack', or for handing out to participants? Is it clear who will be organising the copying of this material, paying for the cost of copying and organising the distribution? What deadline should they be working to?

- Do facilitators know the likely numbers expected for their sessions? Are these agreeable?

- Are the speakers and facilitators aware of where their session fits in to the programme, e.g. who is speaking before and after their session; time, date and location of their session?

- Do the facilitators need to know something about the background, experience, place of work or job titles of their participants?

- Will any facilitators only be present for their own part of the programme? Who should they liaise with?

- Do speakers and facilitators need any background notes, reports or other information to assist them with their preparation?

- Is there a necessity for any of the facilitators to be 'networked' together because, for instance, there is some overlap between the content or themes of their presentations or sessions?

- Are the session facilitators expected to report back on, or write up what went on in, their session? If they are not expected to do so, will this task be undertaken by someone else? Who?

- Have the facilitators agreed to any possible reportage or publication of their material linked to the event? (Try to obtain permission in advance.)

- Finally, make sure one of the organisers has the task of sending out 'thank you' notes to all facilitators and speakers after the event and that they all get their payments on time.

# Checklist 2.12: Speakers'/session leaders' requirements

**Request form from speakers/session organisers for the**

..................................................................... **conference/training event**

Form submitted from ............................................................................................................

Contact me at ......................................................................................................................

Telephone ............................................................................................................................

E-mail ..................................................................................................................................

(Tick boxes and fill in any request details)

I require for my session on ................................................................. the following
items/materials/equipment:

❑  Handout for photocopying. Number of copies................................................................

❑  VHS/DVD or other format video player/recorder (details)

.............................................................................................................................................

❑  Computer equipment/specialist programs (details)

.............................................................................................................................................

❑  Tape/slide equipment ...................................................................................................

❑  Audio equipment ..........................................................................................................

❑  Flip chart, stand and pens ............................................................................................

❑  Overhead projector .......................................................................................................

❑  Tables............... number and size ...............................................................................

Other equipment, for instance, scissors, tape, glue, newspapers, paper, photocopier,
typewriter:

Return form to ....................................................................................................................

## Checklist 2.13: Entertainment

Agree a fee: £............................................   Issue a contract ...........................................

Agree other benefits *(food, drinks, beds)*: ...........................................

Accommodation: ...........................................
*(What is required? Try to negotiate for a 'crash pad' facility for the band with the venue.)*

Travel costs: yes/no and limit: £ ...........................................

Performance and arrival/leaving times: ...........................................

How many in the group/band? ...........................................

Are there any 'friends' coming with them? *(How many are permitted?)*

...........................................

Sound/P.A. requirements: ...........................................

...........................................

Lighting requirements: ...........................................

...........................................

Other *(such as provision of a piano)*: ...........................................

...........................................

## Is this you?

- ● You are optimistic about change in your community.
- ● You are committed to the idea that people are experts in their own lives and have a right to take action on their own behalf.
- ● You believe in social justice, equality and fairness.

## Would you like to...

- ● Take time out to think and reflect on your current practice in a relaxed open learning environment?
- ● Explore ideas and understanding around radical community work practice using a social action framework?

## If so you're an ideal participant for...

# The Centre for Social Action International Summer School

### 23rd – 25th June 2003, Trafford Hall, Chester

www.dmu.ac.uk
DE MONTFORT UNIVERSITY
LEICESTER · BEDFORD

*Centre for Social Action*

Figure 2.2

# Bournemouth University
## Knowledge for business growth presentations

A series of breakfast gatherings to give local business people an opportunity to tap into the wide ranging expertise and guidance available in the county.

| Date | Event | Time | Venue |
|---|---|---|---|
| 8 March | Tax and accounting | 8am - 10.30am | Gillingham |
| 6 May | Environment | 8am - 10.30 am | Wareham |
| 3 June | | | Gillingham |
| 25 May | ICT in your business | 8am - 10.30 am | Portland |
| 12 June | Health | 8am - 10.30 am | Bournemouth |

Tax and accounting    - Review your procedures, best practice
Environment    - Your liability, health & safety, environmental audit, potential savings
ICT in your Business    - Systems audit, specification criteria, e-commerce
Health    - New legislation, current qualifications, strategies for developing staff

To find out more or to register please contact Louise Francis at Bournemouth University on 01202 503999, email s2b@bournemouth.ac.uk or log on to www.bournemouth.ac.uk/s2b/index.html

# Improve your selling techniques and sales performance
### By Reg Bodman, Business Adviser Manager, Business Link Wessex

**Ten Tips to Improve Your Sales Performance**
- Always give your customers a little more than they expect.
- Never say no to your customer - everything is negotiable.
- Make your customers feel good about you, not just your products. People buy from people they like.
- Meet all of your customer's expectations - even if you have to fight your boss over them.
- Do things for your customers that you don't get paid for.
- Know more about your competitor's products than your competitor.
- Make sure you're early for every meeting.
- Dress and present yourself smartly, become an expert in your field.
- Don't sell to your customers, let them buy from you.
- Listen to your customers with your ears and eyes. 55% of all communications are non-verbal, learn to read body language.

**Ten reasons why sales are lost**
- Lack of punctuality.
- Blatant misrepresentation.
- Lack of empathy and understanding.
- Poor listening skills and talking too much.
- Lack of planning and pre-call preparation.
- Inadequate product knowledge.
- Condescending attitude toward the customer.
- Concentrating on yourself or product not the needs of the customer.
- Lack of closing skills.
- Lack of enthusiasm and negative body language.

**Prepared sales people plan to be in the right place at the right time.**
**Tips on closing the deal will be in the next edition of Business Focus.**

page 9

Figure 2.3

Working out arrangements for the administration and financial control of training events can be a very real headache. Most of the people involved in the organisation will be doing so because they are committed to the type of training being offered or to the organisation that is putting the event together. This is particularly true of professional associations and special interest groups, where organising the annual conference can be not just a labour of love, but a threat to sanity and personal relationships as well! Having said that, the sense of pride which organisers can feel when they reach the end of a successful, if frantic, three-day conference for two or three hundred participants, probably rivals the 'buzz' that Eric Clapton or Joni Mitchell feel at the end of a successful concert tour.

## Administration task list

The **administration** process needs to be considered early on in the planning process. All the administrative tasks have a direct relationship to **what needs doing, when, and who should take responsibility**. With a number of the planning and organising groups I have been involved in, we have sat down and 'brainstormed' the likely list of tasks, and then on a flip chart written up the relevant 'who and when' of the equation. Checklist 3.1 (see page 55) is an example of such a task list. I would strongly recommend going through a similar exercise looking at the tasks you will need to undertake and the available personnel.

A lot of the questions which require answering with regard to administration have already been posed in Section 2: *Planning and Preparation*. However, in this section I have tried to add a substantial extra level of detail, which will hopefully help you to grapple with, identify, streamline, and perhaps even enjoy the administrative and financial tasks.

## Using a computer for administration

Nearly every office now houses a substantial resource in the form of computer hardware. Training events can be run more effectively if information is carefully logged, and if the various administrative stages are followed through for each participant, speaker and facilitator. To do this using a computer, you can make effective use of a software program called a database. In the *Office* package that many people have this is called *Access*. This acts as your training event filing system, and, to some extent, actually performs some of the administrative tasks for you. In many offices, you will probably already be using a spreadsheet or accounts software such as *Excel* and *Sage* – these can be useful for managing the financial records. I originally based much of this section on the work Trevor Locke undertook when he worked for NACRO.

To handle the tasks shown in Checklist 3.2 (see page 56), the software programs you use will create record structures, called **fields**, which will meet the needs of your event. A typical range of fields which would meet most requirements is shown in Checklist 3.3 (see page 57). The trick is to make sure that data from application forms, correspondence and telephone messages is transferred quickly and accurately into the database and/or spreadsheet programs. The only danger – and I have suffered from it – are the dreaded 'computer gremlins'. These can turn efficient planning into chaos if the data becomes irretrievable.

**So it is essential to save information carefully onto back-up files on separate discs or other data storage system, and to make frequent hard copies (print-outs) of all your information, just in case of computer failure.**

## Administrative toolkit

Before a training event, in addition to the conference programme and briefing papers for speakers and facilitators, it is worthwhile working out a list of other possible materials that need to be prepared, bought or collected together. It is likely that some information will need to be sent out before the event, and other material could be included as part of a folder or event 'pack'. Checklist 3.4 (see page 58) shows a sample list and a toolkit which might be needed at the event.

## Income from training

If you are planning to organise and 'sell' training, getting your sums right will be a first priority. There are two sides to any balance sheet and perhaps strangely, in 'training', the income side can sometimes get somewhat overlooked amidst the plethora of programme and publicity work, and the administration of applications.

The income from a conference or training event may take a number of forms, which makes the overall costing of an event a bit tricky. Some of the **main sources of training event income** are outlined in Checklist 3.5 (see page 59). They are worth considering by any training organiser, since not all avenues for finance are always looked into.

## Budgets and costings

More and more individuals are now familiar with the concept and organisation of 'business plans'. These are demanded by banks and other financial institutions in order to assess the viability of particular businesses or projects. A training event or conference is exactly the same type of animal and should be subject to as accurate forecasting as possible. What the process of budget planning does is to force training organisers to look at their likely expenditure and income over a given period of time. In simple terms, as in Fig. 3.1, it is possible to make predictions based on different possible levels or income and expenditure. This gives the planning team a better idea of how to set charges, based on their aim either to make a profit or to break even.

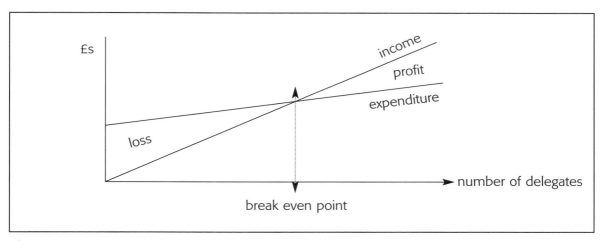

**Figure 3.1**

# Cash flow

This can be a major consideration in any venture. Participant income can be slow in coming through the system, especially when local authorities require invoicing and inordinate lengths of time in which to pay. One option is to insist on payment with bookings. This may mean that some bookings arrive after the closing date, but it could be better than very late payment or non-payment. To achieve the optimum possible cash flow, it is usually best to plan for events as far in advance as possible, advertise early and hope that this secures a good level of advance payments for training places. If it is not possible to cover all advance costs for an event, it will be necessary to run for part of the period on a deficit budget. This will usually entail incurring interest charges for a loan or overdraft. These charges then have to be estimated in the expenditure column for the predicted budget. Cash-flow problems, usually as a result of payment in arrears, have caused the closure of an increasing number of voluntary organisations. Similarly, it can easily 'make or break' a training event or conference. Ignore the subject at your peril!

The costs of running an event fall under two main categories:

1. **Fixed costs**, which will not vary, no matter how many participants there are.
2. **Variable costs**, which vary depending upon the size of the audience and other factors.

There are other costs which are sometimes referred to as **hidden costs**, which are particularly important in people-work training events. These are frequently 'lost' in the overhead budgets of organisations whose staff get involved in organising training and conference events, but, strictly speaking, should be costed in to budgets. Some important items the cost of which you should include in your costings are:

- staff time
- telephones
- postage
- photocopying
- stationery

- heating
- lighting
- use of premises for meetings
- subsistence/food costs
- travel

Your organising group will have to decide whether to include some, or all, of these potentially 'hidden costs' in your budget estimates. Checklist 3.6 (see page 61) can be used for **fixed** and **variable costs** likely to be incurred. You may wish to use or amend it for your event.

## Budget analysis

From the two sets of figures in Checklist 3.6 it is possible to build up predicted and actual budget analysis. A sample format to do this is offered in Checklist 3.7 (see page 62).

## Petty cash

At the event, it is likely that at least one of the organisers will have to walk round with a substantial wad of money in a bag or pocket. Make sure you have calculated the amount you will require for paying hire costs, hospitality, travel, any speakers who require cash in hand and for contingencies. It is also worth checking with the venue to see if they will let you use their safe to keep the money in when it is not needed. You may also need to make an arrangement to bank cash locally.

# Checklist 3.1: A typical administration task list

| Task | Persons responsible | When |
|---|---|---|
| Co-ordinator | Kate | Throughout |
| Bookings | Kate and Jane | April onwards |
| Invoicing and accounts | Kate and Jane | April onwards |
| Venue finding/liaison | Alan and Linda | Immediately |
| Speakers | Jack | Immediately |
| Workshop leaders | Tom and Frank | Immediately |
| Programme/publicity | Alan | Jan/Feb |
| Conference packs | John/Alan | April |
| Briefing papers | Jack, Tom and Frank | From April |
| Entertainment | Gilly and Frank | Jan |
| Catering | Linda | Immediately |
| Media contact | Alan | Jan |
| Registration and badges | Kate and Jane | Conference |
| Rapporteurs | Linda | April |
| Newspaper | Tom, Neil and Alan | Conference |
| Equipment | Tom | April onwards |
| Transport | Jack and Frank | April onwards |
| Exhibition/market place | Gilly and John | April onwards |
| Conference office | Jane | Conference |
| Troubleshooting | Kate, Tom and Alan | Conference |
| Evaluation/conference report | Kate, Alan and Gilly | After conference |

# Checklist 3.2: Computer-based tasks

The types of task for which a computer can be useful include:

- ■ Creating a list of participants' names, organisations, addresses, designation, etc.
- ■ Creating lists of organisers, speakers' and facilitators' names, organisations, addresses and designations.
- ■ Adding special information to the above lists, such as accommodation, workshop details, special diets.
- ■ Monitoring payments, fees, and sending out receipts and invoices.
- ■ Producing address labels for pre-publicity, participants' and organisers' correspondence.
- ■ Producing letters and other 'pro-forma' type material maintaining financial records and monitoring numbers transport requirements.
- ■ Producing badges with name and organisation.

# Checklist 3.3: Record structure for database fields

These could include

| Field | Comment |
|---|---|
| Registration number | It is possible for some programs to generate these automatically |
| Category | Use a key such as: A = admin/organiser<br>S = speaker<br>F = facilitator |
| Surname | |
| Initials/Christian name | |
| Title | Ms/Mrs/Miss/Mr/Dr, etc |
| Position/job | |
| Agency/organisation/ employer | Layout of these address lines needs to produce neat labels for mailings and print outs |
| Address line 1 | |
| Address line 2 | |
| Town | |
| County | |
| Country (if required) | |
| Postcode | |
| Amount due | Must handle the full range of possible payments |
| Amount paid | |
| Receipt number | Must relate to any other accounting systems |
| Invoice number | |
| Event category | e.g. residential, non-residential, subsidised, free etc. |
| Workshop session options | This will relate to choice boxes on the registration form, and should enable sorting out of workshop participant lists |
| Room number | |
| Fees due | |
| Special diets | |
| Special requirements | |
| Transport details (and parking if needed) | |
| Comments | A large-ish field for any additional info |

*Note: Each record structure for a new field must be long enough to accept the maximum amount of information for any entry. This attention to detail will assist with all the other administrative processes, and ease the inevitable problems caused by participants failing to attend, changes in delegates and the myriad other spanners, which get cast into the works.*

## Checklist 3.4: Administrative toolkit

A sample list of materials might consist of:
- event timetable
- a location map of venue and area
- transport information
- workshop and seminar details
- handouts
- a list of participants or organisations
- any related book, reports, statistics

There is also a potentially long list of toolkit items which will be needed at the event. This toolkit can be modified to suit your needs. It might include:
- felt-tip pens
- marker pens
- A4 paper
- card
- blu-tack or similar
- glue (various)
- flipchart pads and stands
- computer and printer (and toner) and possibly scanner
- stapler and staples
- video (and or dvd) and tapes
- audio recorder (cassette or mini disc)
- camera (probably a digital is best)
- screwdriver, and other tools
- plugs and fuses
- receipt book
- first aid box
- extension leads
- petty cash book
- petty cash tin
- petty cash 'float' and change
- sellotape/masking tape
- badges for delegates and spares
- bottle/can/corkscrew
- paper clips
- rulers
- pencils

And, of course, **all the event files and information!**

# Checklist 3.5: Possible sources for training event income

**Participants and their employers**

Few individuals pay for their own training. This means that events and conferences need to meet the perceived needs of employers. They are likely to be looking for:

- value for money

- relevance to the workplace

- priority training skills and knowledge training

- competence accreditation

The pricing of courses and conferences will obviously depend upon the costs incurred by the organisers, but it will also be 'price sensitive', in the sense that different client groups of potential trainees and their employers will have varying budgets and notions of acceptable pricing. So, for instance, a director of social work may think that buying in a trainer for £300 per day is cheap, and they may also baulk at sending a basic grade worker on a three-day conference costing £150. Pricing therefore needs a little 'market research'. Ultimately, the main income line for training events is generated from the participants.

**Grants**

There may be grants available for the whole or part of a training event, or for some of the participants. Sometimes these grants can come from local authorities for specific types of training, especially where it relates to qualifications. The European Social Fund, the Home Office, the Department of Work and Pensions, the Office of the Deputy Prime Minister, the Department for Education all have direct and indirect ways of funding training. This also holds true of many trusts, charities and quasi-autonomous near-government organisations (the infamous quangos). The Directory of Grant-making Trusts, available in many libraries, is a good source of possible funds. The Social Services Year Book is another useful reference source for national and local organisations who might be worth approaching for funding or grant aid.

**Sponsorship**

This is an alternative way of inviting financial support for an event. Some commercial firms, as well as trade and professional organisations, will support training events and conferences. Depending upon your field, it is worth constructing a list of organisations that might consider some level of backing for your event. National and local training organisations may themselves not have enough personnel to put on all the training they would like to, and therefore may be in the market to subsidise other events. Specialist journals and magazines frequently offer this type of support and are worth at least a phone call.

To 'sell' this idea to potential sponsors, make a list of the positive benefits of involvement in your event. These are likely to include media/professional profile; spin-off credibility; value-for-money of involvement.

→

59

**Checklist 3.5 contd…**

Some organisations/companies will sponsor or fund certain parts of a training event, so think about what extra facilities you want to lay on. This can range from the production and printing of special folders and/or notepads, through to the provision of a crèche, a computer for administration, transport, the costs of the conference report, or a 'free bar' for an hour!

### Exhibitions/market place
Many companies wish to have a presence at training events, especially where their product or services are directly relevant to the majority of the participants and where the participants may be budget-holders. Selling space at an event may be a relatively easy and painless way of getting 'value-added' revenue.

### Training materials/books/reports
This area can be lucrative. You may consider organising a bookstall, or producing and selling a conference report or a set of conclusions/findings. Another option is to build these items into the overall charge to participants, but as a way of cross-subsidising the production of valuable training materials. Some training events are even specifically organised around the launch of a new book or report. Many participants will buy sensibly priced materials if they feel that they will be of use once they return to base, either for themselves or colleagues. Providing invoices after the event may encourage sales!

### Add-on components
Some training events have the capacity for add-on events which can have an income-generating capacity in their own right. It may be that the main plenary could attract a large paying audience, or perhaps the entertainment could be charged for additionally. If an event is part of a series, this may generate a useful income flow. Consider whether it is worth selling the event as part of a package, at a suitable 'discount'.

### Advertising
Some conferences earn money from advertising in their programmes, offering inserts in training packs, banners and hoardings at the venue. A further way of earning can come from selling label runs of participants' names and addresses, although this raises some ethical questions and problems under the Data Protection Act.

# Checklist 3.6: Fixed and variable costs

Checklist for ................................................................................................ training event

to be held on.......................................................... at ........................................................

## Fixed costs

| | | | |
|---|---|---|---|
| Use of venue | £................. | Speakers' fees | £................. |
| Workshop leader's fees | £................. | Marketing costs (advertising, leaflet, postage, insertions) | £................. |
| Organisers' costs/fees | £................. | Admin, secretarial | £................. |
| Equipment hire/purchase | £................. | Printing, copying | £................. |
| Training packs/folders | £................. | Badges | £................. |
| Exhibition/market place | £................. | Insurance, legal, accounts | £................. |
| Transport | £................. | Interest charges | £................. |
| Disaster/contingency fund | £................. | Signs, stage set, PA system | £................. |
| Conference report | £................. | | |

## Variable costs

| | | | |
|---|---|---|---|
| Accommodation for participants | £................. | Catering | £................. |
| Entertainment (various) | £................. | Petty cash | £................. |
| Variable admin. costs | £................. | | |

# Checklist 3.7: Budget analysis (actual/estimated)

For ............................................................................................ training event

| Income | | Expenditure | |
|---|---|---|---|
| Exhibition | £.............. | Equipment | £.............. |
| Sponsors | £.............. | Organisers | £.............. |
| Subsidies | £.............. | Entertainment | £.............. |
| Publications | £.............. | Report publishing | £.............. |
| Other | £.............. | Travel | £.............. |
| Other | £.............. | Interest | £.............. |
| Other | £.............. | Exhibition | £.............. |
| Other | £.............. | Other | £.............. |
| | | Other | £.............. |
| | | Other | £.............. |
| *Income Total* | £.............. | *Expenditure Total* | £.............. |
| *Less expenditure* | £.............. | | |
| **Profit/loss =** | £.............. | | |

**Notes:**
VAT is not included in these calculations but will have to be charged by organisations which are VAT registered. Charities have special VAT status and are usually zero-rated. It is worth checking this area out with your accountant or with VAT inspectors, who are usually very helpful. A number of spaces for 'other' are included in order for it to be tailored to your needs.

# Section 4    Styles of Training Event

The material presented in this section is not intended to pre-empt the style in which your training event or conference is organised. The section offers some ideas and models for the overall structure and style of the event and some suggestions for methods which can be employed by individual facilitators and workshop leaders. Initially, in setting the **aims and theme** of the event, the organisers will be establishing the framework for the possible styles of presentation and organisation. For instance, the organising group may decide that a conference is not going to be dominated by themes and issues, but, instead, should be geared to developing the personal skills of the participants. I have also been involved in planning a number of training events that offer different strands, so that there were policy workshops for senior managers and elected officers, and practice-oriented workshops for practitioners and part-time staff.

## Styles and methods

The sorts of questions which should be considered before deciding which styles and methods to employ will probably include those set out in Checklist 4.1 (see page 73).

In looking at the style of the event, the level of formality will be one consideration. The conference of the British Medical Association has a formal meal, and dinner jackets are obligatory. At most other times, delegates wear suits and listen to speeches in a large lecture theatre. This can be contrasted with the training events run by less formal organisations and associations such as Youth and Policy Journal, the Housing Studies Association or the Critical Social Policy collective. These types of organisations are likely to bring together a mixture of academics and practitioners who tend to demand participative structures and workshops. Other conferences such as the annual housing conference at Harrogate, mixes exhibitions with formal and informal presentations. The organisers' choice of style, or the mixture of styles, will depend upon some implicit aims and objectives, which are not always synonymous with the aims stated on the training publicity, and may even conflict with them. These may include ensuring that as far as possible, all participants are:

- Actively involved.
- More confident and independent.
- More motivated towards their work
- Able to apply skills and knowledge learned back in the workplace.
- Less critical of their employing organisation or colleagues.
- More aware of colleagues' and consumers' needs and opinions.
- Likely to leave with an improved level of morale (thereby decreasing staff turnover).
- Offered opportunities to improve promotion chances and career advancement.
- Able to consider further training opportunities.
- Able to accept the 'messages' built into the training/conference.

Effective training depends upon the capacity of the participants to learn, their willingness to learn and participate; their motivation; the organisational methods used in the training process; and finally the skill and ability of the trainer or facilitator. The styles of organisation and methods used should maximise this effectiveness. Later, in the 'Evaluation' section of the book, I offer some models and methods for measuring and monitoring learning and the success of events. In people-work training, it seems important that training should embody the:

- Sharing of ideas, opinions, experience – and mistakes!
- Building on strengths of participants.
- Allowing for flexibility in the programme.
- Encouraging of the improvement of consumer services and their participation in decision-making.

# Training styles

There is an inevitable link between the **style of presentation** and the **method of presentation**. Both are really part of the overall style, since the form of presentation, a plenary or workshop, for instance, and the method of delivery, is inextricably bound together. To clarify what I am meaning by the terms: I am using the **style of presentation** to initially describe the preferred **format**, and then I will describe under **methods** some of the options available to presenters. Styles for consideration in designing and organising a training event or conference include the following:

## *Plenaries*

These are large meetings, often involving speeches and presentations. Because they can, potentially, alienate participants as well as inform them, a first question is, should there be any plenaries? And then, what balance of time should be spent in them?

Plenaries usually offer ideas, opinions and information, and can utilise other resources such as video and overhead projection equipment. Plenaries offer the opportunity to set the scene at a conference. They can also establish an agenda for action in subsequent components of an event. In people-work training, they frequently involve much more involvement for participants, even to the extent of encouraging interruptions and feedback during inputs from speakers. More formal plenaries may either disallow contributions from the 'floor', or can formalise these by asking for written questions in advance, calling for responses from speakers or panel members. Other possibilities include the chair asking for all contributors to signal their intention to speak through the chair, or coming out to join some sort of 'queue' system. Plenaries can also make use of a 'roving microphone' which requires at least two assistants with radio microphones, or microphones attached to long, flexible cables which can be manoeuvred to where the participants are sitting. When getting participants to ask questions, or make their own opinions heard, it is usually a good idea to invite them to state who they are and were they come from, or their place of work. In the formal 'closed session' of a trade union or professional membership association, the agenda and items for debate and voting will usually have been prepared well in advance and circulated in printed form to all attendees. The style of these presentations involves more ritual. It is usual for there to be a proposer and seconder and then other contributors are invited to speak for, and against, a motion or candidate, before the chair moves the meeting to a vote. This type of meeting always requires careful minuting. With conferences and training events where keynote or very original speeches are being made, it is worth considering whether it is useful to video or tape the inputs.

In plenaries, 'being heard' is of vital importance. Therefore, a good public address system is nearly always required. This throws up its own problems if speakers feel inhibited by having their voices amplified and by having to use a microphone. In large-scale venues, it is often necessary to use extra TV/video screens for audiences farther back in the auditorium. Sometimes this even involves networking different venues or participants together, using conference paging, Internet or TV link-ups, but these very sophisticated systems are a bit beyond the scope of this book.

Plenaries also have a 'boredom factor'. **Talking heads**, as speakers at conferences are often referred to, need to have something to contribute, and to have the ability to convey their message with clarity and as succinctly as possible. When organising a programme, it is useful to space out 'plenaries' with workshops and other more participative forms of working in between. It is generally agreed that the usual maximum length for any input to maintain interest from an audience is somewhere between 40 minutes and an hour. So, by including feedback and questions, an hour and a half, or an hour and three-quarters is about the maximum length for a single plenary to remain effective. In a conference, or in a training event with a message, it is usual to start the event with a plenary and finish with the same gathering of the participants. This can give a sense of cohesion to the event, but it can also prove dangerous, potentially sending the participants away on a 'low', if the event has been long and tiring, if the last plenary is slow or boring, or if the participants are itching to get home, and start drifting away throughout the final session!

The other significant type of plenary session is the 'self-organised' event, which may be a last minute affair, participant-led, and focused on the needs and interests of people with particular common interests. In the larger conferences, these fringe events allow the level of flexibility demanded by many participants, who like the freedom to have a 'space' within the event to offer their own forms of training or information/debate session. They can also provide useful forums for the 'real' issues and views of participants to be aired. In events I have been involved in, these more spontaneous events have often been organised by women's and men's groups, people from particular geographical areas, and particular ethnic groups.

The organisation of the seating for a plenary can affect the way in which an input is received. In some cases, the seating is fixed, as in a theatre or lecture hall auditorium. Even then, organisers should consider carefully whether all the seats should be used, or whether, because of sound or vision constraints, some seats should be ruled out. The recommended angle out from the speakers to the audience for visibility and intelligibility is approximately 60 degrees, as in Figure 4.1.

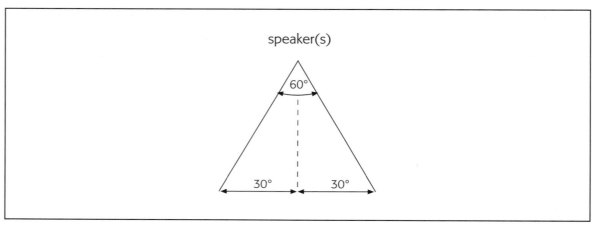

**Figure 4.1**

When the seating is fixed, it may cause problems for any disabled participants, and organisers should consider other options to this in advance.

If seating can be moved around, the angle, shape, aisles, space between chairs and distance from the presenters can all be varied as in Figure 4.2.

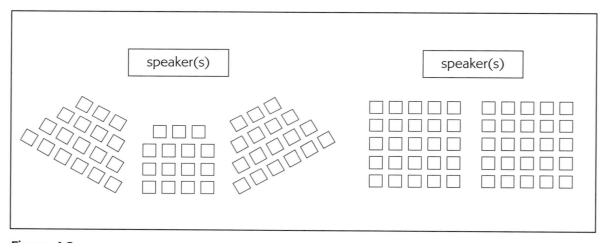

**Figure 4.2**

It is particularly advantageous to have seating which is flexible when the organisers need to use the same space for a variety of different types of presentation, or, on occasions, where a presenter uses a mixture of methods. For instance, in one large youth event, after a few 'hellos' from the stage, we used a sequence of mass participation exercises. This was followed by dividing the entire audience into small groups, and then we invited everyone back into a 'plenary' session. Because it broke the ice and was somewhat unexpected, it seemed to work well.

Finally, it is worth remembering that a large plenary may require a number of organisers or facilitators and assistants. It is worth looking at the potential roles, perhaps using Checklist 4.2 (see page 74) which you can modify:

### Role of chairperson

The role of chairperson in plenaries is also worthy of consideration. This person can help to make any speakers and presenters feel comfortable or threatened, and it is often the introduction from the chair that establishes the reception for, and the tone of, the input. The chairperson will need a clear **briefing** from the event organisers, for instance, as in Checklist 4.3 (see page 75).

### Facilitation

The main reason for having a chairperson is to **facilitate** the smooth and effective running of a plenary, and to improve information flow. It is usually best if the chairperson keeps out of debate as far as possible, and delegates that function, if more active involvement in debate is required. Add a sense of humour and an appropriate level of empathy and you most probably have the recipe for a good chairperson. I've added a short list below of positive and negative effects of good facilitation. These apply equally to discussion group and workshop leaders.

| The pros – if it's working | The cons – if it's failing |
| :---: | :---: |
| enabling | de-skilling |
| creative | alienating |
| targeted | unfocused |
| relevant | irrelevant |
| stimulating | de-motivating |
| challenging | boring |
| participative | authoritarian |
| planned | disorganised |
| well-run | poorly-run |

### Small group sessions

These tend to form the heart and the soul of many training events and courses. The names for these smaller groupings vary, depending upon the profession and the training background of the organisers. As briefly mentioned in the Glossary at the beginning of this book, some of the most common are:

- workshop
- seminar
- work team or group
- special interest group
- skill-practice group
- buzz or cluster group
- think-tank
- discussion group

Within each model or style of group, as previously mentioned, various methods of preparation and presentation can be employed, some of which are described in the final part of this section, after a little more information on how the different styles of small group sessions may work.

One of the essentials of working effectively in small groups is choosing the correct **maximum size** for the group. When organisers are preparing the programme for a training event, they must liaise very closely with those people they are inviting to lead or run small group sessions. A major factor will be setting the limits for each small group. Checklist 4.1 (see page 73) should be of some use in providing a checklist for group leaders, but it is equally essential to ensure that the group will be small enough to offer everyone a supportive and creative learning environment.

Another major factor which must be carefully thought about by the group facilitator is: **How best can my topic or subject area be presented?** Providing practical skill sessions on the use of computers, or video work with community groups, is very different from running a planning and policy-making session on implementing community care. So, **what** you are trying to teach or discuss should fit in with **who** you are going to do it with, **where** it will take place, and **why** you are doing it anyway. Taken together this should help to determine the **How-to-do-it.** (*Note:* My thanks are due to my erstwhile colleagues in Scotland: Jeremy Wyatt, Alex Williamson, Tim Holmes and Ken Hamilton. They helped me produce a set of notes on *Running Workshops or Making Presentations*. It's now out of print, but it provided the genesis for much of what follows.)

## Small group types

There are many differing opinions on what should, and does, go on in **small group training sessions**. The very terms 'workshop', 'discussion group' and the like, are frequently the cause of problems as organisers and participants fail to understand, or agree with, each other's expectations. The onus is on the conference organisers, working with, and through the group facilitators, to find the most appropriate methods and styles to suit the subject matter, the participants and the occasion.

Structuring the small group sessions requires looking at the possible processes and methods that might be employed and then using the best vehicle to 'run' them in. The group organiser must understand the overall intention and aims of the event and the organisers' goals, and then, by properly planning and preparing, do their utmost to identify and meet the needs of the group participants. One of the worst offences of any group facilitator at a people-work event is to use small group sessions to 'show off' their own level of knowledge. This approach will usually fail to impress and is unlikely to improve the skill levels of the group participants. Returning to the oft-quoted 'horses for courses' phrase, the choice of small group type must be suitable for the job in hand. The small group facilitator will often know more about the subject under review than many of the participants, but working in small groups should be fundamentally about participation and empowerment. Group leaders should therefore be conscious of the effect that they may have on a group as a result of the choice of style and methods of presentation.

## Seminars

These are more regularly used on courses involving students training for professional qualifications than at conferences and training events. The standard format is for one or more students to make a presentation, which is followed by a detailed discussion both of the 'paper' and of the issues raised. It is usually a structured setting which should encourage participation, but there is likely to be at least one 'expert' present who will regulate the running of the seminar, and may make some pronouncements on the presentation and the subject under discussion. The seminar group will usually meet together on a regular basis over a period of time and can become a 'work/team group' once they have become familiar with one another and confident of each other.

## Discussion groups

These are usually facilitated and may involve some sort of short input to get the ball rolling. The facilitator may need to encourage participants to get to know one another, so that they can explore topics more fully and exchange views. In a conference or training event, they are frequently utilised to expand on themes and subjects already raised in plenary inputs. The group may be required to produce ideas and comments for sharing back into the main event or plenary and can require someone to act as spokesperson for the group. The facilitator must ensure that all who wish to offer views are encouraged to do so, and prevent anyone in the group monopolising the proceedings.

## Workshops, work and team groups

These are meant to be more task-focused. Often they are designed to improve participants' skills, make recommendations for action, or focus attention on particular problems. The range of application is enormous and they are probably the most frequently used and complex of the small group session types. The leader or facilitator needs to be especially careful that they have adequately prepared an appropriate programme of material and sequences. Workshops tend to be of longer duration (usually at least one and a half hours) and may meet more than once in the context of a longer training event. If the focus of attention is on a professional or geographical 'problem', a particular work team, or inter-agency/professional grouping, this may determine the membership for the workshop. Role-plays, games, simulations and brainstorming are just some of the techniques which may be employed within workshops.

## Buzz or cluster groups

These are used as a way of getting participants involved and working together. They are also useful in generating quick and spontaneous ideas. The most common model is for between three and six participants to be allocated into a buzz group for a short period of time (5, 10, 15 minutes). In this grouping they address a topic, for instance, who should we be prioritising our work with? Or, how do we tackle racism in our workplace? All the groups would then usually report back their particular views and ideas into a larger group for further discussion, and perhaps for some sort of action plan.

## Skill-practice groups

Most of the time this type of group would come under the umbrella heading of the workshop, but on occasions it will be useful to design group sessions with a heavy emphasis on practice skills. Skill areas such as counselling; relationship games; use of computers; first aid; video and photography; arts and craft activities are typical of these types of workshops. Specialist techniques used by some practitioners in the broad spectrum of social services, such as transactional analysis and the Alexander technique are also possible for inclusion into this type of group session, but, in these cases, the overall nature of the training event is likely to be focused around some sort of related theme such as 'empowerment'.

### Think-tanks

This type of grouping is established to generate new ideas and solutions. They are less used within training events, and are more often organised as a way of providing a 'sounding-board' for an organisation or individual who needs advice and information. The tasks can vary from trying to find solutions to problems such as vandalism and anti-social behaviour on a particular estate, through to advising on 'training needs' for a local authority.

### Special interest groups

At conferences, organisers often programme-in particular information-giving or experience-sharing group sessions which will bring together participants with particular interests, perspectives or skills. These can also offer the opportunity for the participant-led workshop. In this way, in a general conference on improving child care, there could be special interest sessions for participants who wanted to explore in more depth the implications of work with under-5s, or work in multi-ethnic communities. Organisers of training programmes can become more proactive about this, and encourage participants to indicate on their booking form 'other workshops' they would like to see run at the event.

One of the important considerations is to get the balance right between listening and doing, and work and leisure. Many training events are over-programmed and do not allow participants enough time to reflect on their own experience, or to fully utilise the opportunity of 'being away' from the daily workplace. Much debate and 'real' work does happen in the more flexible and less formal settings of participative workshops.

## Methods of presentation

In the final part of this section, there are ideas for some of the **sequences, exercises** and **methods of presenting** material in training events which are particularly relevant to group session organisers. Many other books exist on developing training skills, some of which are listed in the *Resources* section at the back of this book. There are many others specifically focusing on the use of games, simulations, role-plays, and audio-visual aids. This brief section is intended only to present a taster of the sort of options which are available, and must be carefully considered by event organisers and by those charged with running specific group sessions.

One particular consideration in people-work training is to create the most conducive environment for mutual learning. Agreeing the boundaries and rules for a group session is an important and useful part of the process. The **safeguards** rules offered in Checklist 4.4 (see page 76) can be used with a group at the outset as a means of establishing a shared ownership for the training, and as a way of creating a training environment where participants will feel comfortable, caring and cared for, as well as hopefully being challenged and stimulated. (The suggested safeguards are reprinted from *Effective use of Teambuilding in Social Welfare Organisations*, Alan Dearling.)

### *Attitudinal and aptitudinal training*

At risk of labouring the point, I would like to repeat here that **methods of training must be matched up appropriately with the aims of event organisers and participants' needs**.

Much training is said to be:

**Attitudinal:** looking at ways in which attitudes can be challenged and possibly changed.

and

**Aptitudinal:** looking at methods whereby skills can be improved and services delivered more effectively.

The framework for undertaking this training – if you like, the **value base** – can be examined in more detail through using the following section and the Checklist 4.5 (see page 77).

# Training methods

Training methods may be:

- **Informative:** offering ideas, information and descriptions.
- **Controlling/managing:** directive, by exerting pressure and power over the participants.
- **Proactive:** by challenging and actively encouraging participants to engage in the training experience.
- **Reactive:** through responding to the requests and information generated by the participants.

This model is a bit stark and too black and white. Most training mixes the methods used, and the aims tend to be fudged. There is also a problem sometimes in terms of contradictory expectations of training between trainers, participants, managers and funders. This is worth keeping in the back of one's mind when organising packages of training. It has also become even more apparent as more training gets linked to on-the-job assessment, accreditation and supervised practice.

My own personal, professional commitment is to training methods which as far as possible encourage and develop **both the personal and professional potential of staff members**. Therefore, training methods need to address how best some of the following can be improved relative to personal and professional requirements.

Training methods should encourage:

- appropriate attitudes
- empathy
- understanding
- self-knowledge
- acquisition of technical and practical skills

- improved care skills
- better management and administration
- confidence building
- enabling practices
- partnership working
- the growth of citizenship and empowerment
- anti-sexist and anti-racist practices

Checklist 4.5 (see page 77) outlines some of the potential methods for use in small group sessions of different kinds. The training needs of the various organisations in the people-services vary tremendously, and it is impossible to predict every possible type of training sequence that could be used. The contrasts can be enormous. Think, for instance, of the differences between a training event based at an outdoor adventure centre, using abseiling, canoeing and a survival adventure on an uninhabited island, compared with a one-day, lecture-based, management training seminar located in a Holiday Inn. Yet, on further reflection, both events might legitimately claim to be about teambuilding!

What is also true is that some methods of training are transferable from one setting to another using a little imagination, flexibility and some modification. As an example, one of my personal favourites amongst teambuilding activities is the use of various forms of **urban trail**. These encourage teamwork, observation and curiosity. They are based on a mixture of orienteering and a kind of urban treasure trail. Training methods are nothing if not diverse.

You might wish to use the Checklist 4.5 as the basis for an exercise with some of the members of the training planning group to see what methods are most appropriate for the programme being planned. Remind facilitators that they should avoid using training methods and styles which they are not familiar with. Trainees are not guinea pigs!

## Engaging a trainer

Throughout this book, the accent is on identifying appropriate styles of learning. In the people-services, more and more training is taking place in multi-agency teams and it increasingly involves consumers as well as staff members. The methods and styles of training need to be amended to accommodate this change. In particular, more and more forms of experiential learning, based around the lives, experiences and strengths and weaknesses of participants, are being designed.

To facilitate this, trainers must cut down on talk-and-chalk routines and lengthy presentations, and, instead, encourage much more practical activity. Learning by talking, involvement and doing is central to good participative learning. So, finally in this section, I have included as Checklist 4.6 (see page 80), a very useful summary on engaging a trainer, which is slightly modified from *Developing Training Skills* (Pickles et al.).

# Checklist 4.1: Questions to determine the style and methods employed in training

- Are there specific tasks to be tackled?

- Are certain results (learning outcomes), such as the building of skills, knowledge acquisition, affective (emotional) learning, or attitude change seen as the intended outcome(s)?

- Do the staff have similar knowledge or training backgrounds? Are there likely to be a range of expectations amongst the participants? What are they? How can they be provided for in a mutually compatible way?

- Are the likely ages, sexual composition, cultural backgrounds and sexual preferences of participants of any relevance to the style of the event and the methods employed?

- Is the maintenance of confidentiality a concern?

- Do boundaries and safeguards need to be established?

- Are statements of intent on anti-sexist and anti-racist approaches required?

- Are there any policy or mission statements from the organisations backing the event that must be built in to the programme?

- Is the training connected with any particular discipline or training approach, e.g. experiential learning, transactional analysis, NLP, social action, action centred, directive or non-directive learning? Does everyone involved with the event understand these approaches?

- Are there any known resistances to training? What are they?

- What strengths and weaknesses amongst the participants can be built upon or rectified?

- Is the event intended to overcome any conflicts or disputes?

- Is there a need to provide support for work teams? Are there any issues relating to line management problems?

- Where do the participants normally work? Will they be expected to work in teams or in any collective way after the event?

- Are there ways in which the event can be used to increase the motivation of the participants?

- Does the size or scale of the event determine style and methods available as options?

- Is any accreditation and assessment of participants taking place?

# Checklist 4.2: Plenary roles

Possible organisational roles include:

- chairperson
- minute-taker/rapporteur
- microphone assistant
- lighting/audio-visual technician
- panel members/presenter
- trouble-shooter
- audio or video recorder

# Checklist 4.3: Chairperson's briefing

This briefing may need to include information on:

- Aims and intended outcomes.
- Accurate and appropriate material and information on speakers and contributors.
- Information on the timing and programme of the plenary.
- Additional practical information for the participants.
- Written notes for their own contribution (welcome/expression of pleasure, etc.).
- Any practical back-up on resources, audio-visual aids, drinks for speakers, etc.

The chairperson of a meeting or plenary should also consider:

- What personal style to adopt?
- How best to assist anyone who may feel threatened?
- How to control anyone who gets 'out of hand'?
- Whether issues need to be agreed or voted upon?
- Whether there is a particular objective or set of aims?
- How to keep an eye on a clock?
- How to watch the audience and try and gauge their reactions to the inputs?
- How to clarify points made and identify issues where necessary?
- How to encourage debate and aid decision-making?
- How to keep things moving, and speakers to the point? (And do the same yourself!)

# Checklist 4.4: Safeguards

*(Note: facilitators must be familiar with this material)*

While we are together in this staff development training, it will be useful if we agree some ground rules. You are free to disagree with any which are on this sheet, and to suggest others which the group may like to adopt.

## Safeguards

■ Detailed information on issues raised in discussion should not be discussed outside of this group.

■ Participants make their own decisions on how far they are willing to share personal information, beliefs, etc. with other group members.

■ Everyone is entitled to their own views, attitudes, opinions.

■ Anyone is entitled to challenge these in a positive and supportive way.

■ Anyone can decide not to participate in an exercise if they wish.

■ It is expected that any views which the group feel are sexist or racist will be challenged by group members and the facilitator.

## Role of the facilitator

The facilitator should encourage participants to:

■ Work together in a positive and creative way.

■ Share experiences from their own work and lives.

■ Participate in as much of the group teambuilding activity as possible.

■ Challenge sexism and racism.

■ Work within the safeguards, especially concerning confidentiality.

Additionally, the organiser of the sessions will facilitate the group to make its own safeguards and rules. Participants can also be invited to suggest a process for changing and reviewing the rules of the group. Some individuals may have different sensitivities than others, and the facilitator should enable these to be explored in a caring and supportive manner.

You may, for instance, wish to discuss when you want to take breaks, and whether you want a rule about smoking.

The facilitator may wish to explore the issue of how people in groups or teams can act destructively, by asking the group:

*How might you work to sabotage the group if you felt like doing so?*

# Checklist 4.5: Training methods

**Written exercises**

The most popular forms of these, because they are quick to complete, are various forms of attitude (or attitudinal) survey forms or questionnaires. These can be used to focus attention on current attitudes, skills, beliefs and knowledge levels of participants. Some of the same types of forms can also be used in assessing and evaluating the effectiveness of training inputs. One example of what is called a **semantic differential test** follows. These can be useful in encouraging staff to reflect on their own performance. (If you construct these, make sure you mix up the characteristics on the right and left hand sides of the grid.) They are particularly useful as an exercise to be run before and after specific 'attitude changing' course inputs.

*Example – semantic differential test*

At work, you feel that you are:
*(Place an 'x' along each line at the point that most accurately reflects your self-view.)*

| | | |
|---|---|---|
| well motivated | I...........I...........I...........I...........I...........I | poorly motivated |
| popular | I...........I...........I...........I...........I...........I | unpopular |
| a loner | I...........I...........I...........I...........I...........I | part of a team |
| unambitious | I...........I...........I...........I...........I...........I | ambitious |
| conservative | I...........I...........I...........I...........I...........I | radical |
| settled | I...........I...........I...........I...........I...........I | unsettled |
| tolerant | I...........I...........I...........I...........I...........I | intolerant |

(*Note:* careful analysis of results is important, especially if it used more than once, since a seemingly negative movement in an individual's response may mean that they are being more honest than in the first test.)

**Case studies**

These may be offered in written or verbal form, or through tape or video presentations. The aim is to present examples of practice which will allow analysis, consideration of possible solutions and identification of various choices of action. Good case studies must be prepared in advance, and if possible tested for glitches. If the participants come from a mixture of backgrounds, case studies which are relevant for all may be hard to design. There may also be problems if some of the group are not as literate as others.

→

**Checklist 4.5 contd…**

### Simulations

These create a 'real' or 'imaginary' world or situation. Participants are then invited to participate in it. Some simulations are based on role-plays of real-life work situations. Others can represent involvement in 'other worlds' or communities, or offer multiple choices as in survival exercises, based anywhere from the Arctic to the Moon. Many simulations help participants to develop their decision-making and team-working skills. They can be a lot of fun, but some participants will opt out because a simulation may appear to be 'threatening' or uncomfortable.

### Games

These come in all sorts of forms. Some are what is called, in the social services training world, 'relationship games'. These allow participants to express their feelings, opinions and emotions. Some may feature activities and action, some, paper and pencils and others may encourage new uses for old favourites like darts, pool and dominoes. Games can often break down barriers and inhibitions and enable individuals to find new confidence in relationships. For workers, this is equally important, as a lot of work problems are to do with inter-personal disagreements. Games can help resolve some of these blocks. With my friend and colleague, Howie Armstrong, I have compiled two compendiums of such games and sequences: *The New Youth Games Book* and *World Youth Games*. Although 'youth' is in the title of both, they have been extensively used by trainers for 'youths' of all ages!

### Role-plays

Participants are given roles to play in work-related or other scenarios. They then act out these roles, which can be watched by other participants or videoed. Role-plays can be powerful tools in helping staff to 'feel' what their service customers experience, or to develop an understanding of what other professionals' jobs involve. Once again, some participants find participation difficult, and any individuals with learning difficulties or handicaps will need sensitive assistance. There can also be problems with participants coming out of roles, which can create tension and resistance to training immediately following the role-play.

### Ice-breakers

These help to relax participants and break down inhibitions. Often they involve a fairly lively game which can be used to start off either small or large training groups. They help participants get to know one another and relieve anxieties. Some involve varying levels of physical touching, and others help group members develop trust in each other.

### Brainstorming

This is a fairly simple technique for use by a facilitator to try and generate as many new ideas on a given subject in the shortest possible time. Problems, setting aims, situations can all be addressed in this way, and the aim is to produce a quick list of 'possible' ideas which are not evaluated initially, but, after a short, limited time, they can be discussed and prioritised or even acted upon if appropriate.

→

**Checklist 4.5 contd…**

**Audio-visual aids**
The range of video, film, computer, tape-slide, audio tapes and overhead projection slides all offer useful presentational devices for workshop or group session leaders. As with other methods, the planning, preparation and selection of well-made and relevant materials is the key.

**Handouts**
Written notes and reprints can usefully be presented as photocopied handouts to participants, as long, of course, that you are not infringing copyright! It is frequently best to give them out in advance of a particular workshop so that they are read before the group meets.

**Critical incident analysis**
This technique involves participants in identifying areas of their working lives which have presented problems. They then try to work out alternative solutions, ultimately with the assistance of other group members and the facilitator.

**Other exercises**
Specific exercises can be devised to address the needs of particular groups. Some may be task oriented; others can confront problems and seek solutions. For instance, in a work group the team leader may be falling out with other team members. One exercise which is sometimes useful is to pair the team leader off with another member of the team and ask them to write a short list of the three things they like most about each other, and then three suggestions for change they would most like to see in the other person. They then share the suggestions and discuss the points raised.

## Checklist 4.6: Engaging a trainer

It is very unlikely that an in-house trainer will be able to meet all the training needs of a particular organisation. At such times the organisation should look to other trainers for the skills or knowledge to run particular training events. This checklist is divided into three sections:

### 1. What to cover before commissioning the trainer

You need to be as clear as possible in your own mind about what you require. If you want a trainer for a particularly important, expensive or sensitive training event, you should consider the selection of the correct trainer in the same way as you would if you were recruiting a new member of staff.

This will entail having the equivalent of an accurate **job description** (in this case, a description of the training tasks to be undertaken). You should also have a **person specification** for the trainer (a clear statement about the essential skills, experience and attitudes which you are looking for). Remember that just as you would not engage a new staff member who did not meet all your essential criteria, so you should also avoid engaging a trainer who does not meet the key criteria you have determined. It is far less damaging to delay a training event than have one run by someone who is incompetent or unsuitable. Things you need to consider include:

- *What is the purpose of the training event?*
  What do you want the training event to cover. What are the reasons for looking outside the organisation for a trainer? Is this a response to a need identified by potential participants? Could there be any reluctant attendees? Are there any other ways in which you could help people achieve the learning outcomes (e.g. visits, directed reading, supervision)?

- *Who is the target group for the training evening?*
  Will this be a self-selecting group which responds to your marketing of the event, or will the participants be selected by others? How many people will be involved? What is their range of experience, interest and motivation?

- *What, precisely, do you want people to learn as a result of the training event?*
  How clear are you about this? How much say in the outcomes will participants have before and during the event? Who else do you need to consult about outcomes (e.g. managers, users of services)?

- *What sort of training approach do you want the trainer to use?*
  Are the participants familiar or more comfortable with a particular approach? What will their expectations be? What kind of methods would you like to see used?

- *What about dates and venues?*
  When do you want the event to happen? Are there any particular time constraints? Remember about school holidays, religious and other holidays, etc. Where will the event be held? Make sure the venue is accessible.

→

**Checklist 4.6 contd...**

■ *What is your budget?*
How much can you spend on the trainer's fees, venue hire, travel expenses, resource material, meals, accommodation and all the other expenses involved? Do you have the authority to negotiate fees and expense payments with the trainer?

## 2. What to discuss with the trainer

If at all possible you should arrange a meeting with the trainer to discuss the proposed training event. This may not be necessary if you already know the trainer, but is essential if you have not worked with the person before. It is important to allow as much opportunity as possible for the trainer to talk about their ideas for the event. What they ask you, and, more importantly, what they overlook, may be useful indicators of their thoroughness and suitability for the job. A good trainer will anticipate most of the questions in this checklist. If they do not, it is even more important that you are satisfied with their answers to your questions. Things you should ask the trainer include:

■ *Is the trainer able to work to your brief?*
What is their previous experience of work in this area? Look at any material they have used in previous training events of this sort. How does it compare with what you and the participants are after? Get some questions from participants about the subject area. See how the trainer responds to these. Are they prepared to be honest with you about what they don't know?

■ *How would the trainer plan to organise the training event?*
What methods would they use? To what extent do these methods fit in with the goals of the event and the expectations of the participants? To what extent would they negotiate with the participants over outcomes and methods? What is their attitude to the participants?

■ *What is the trainer's value base?*
Do they have experience of working with personal social services? What are their views about equality of opportunity? How do they tackle this in practice? How do they encourage participation in their training events?

■ *What does the trainer charge?*
What are their fees? What does this include? Ask specifically about preparation time, handouts and other resource materials, travel and other expenses, VAT, and administration costs. Do their rates change according to numbers attending? What do they charge for postponement or cancellation? Do these penalty clauses also apply to the trainers in cases of their own cancellation? In some large training organisations, you cannot assume that the negotiator will also be the trainer. Find out if the person you are negotiating with will be the person who undertakes the training.

→

**Checklist 4.6 contd…**

■ *Is the trainer available and interested?*
Check times and dates. Will the proposed venue be acceptable? How much time will they need for preparation? Ask them to send a proposal with a programme for the event, but only if you think you might be prepared to engage them. (Producing proposals can be extremely time-consuming. It is unfair to ask a trainer to spend what may well be unpaid time producing a proposal if you do not have any intention of engaging them.)

■ *How will the event be evaluated?*
What kind of evaluation do you want of the event? What ideas does the trainer have about evaluation? Who will undertake the evaluation? What role (if any) will the trainer have in undertaking the evaluation? Do you plan to evaluate the trainer's performance? If so, how will this be done?

**3. Debriefing the trainer after the event**
We include the third section because, as an organiser of training and a trainer yourself, there may be a lot you can learn from discussing and evaluating the event you have planned with the trainer you engage. This can help you to improve your own training skills and help you to avoid pitfalls the next time you commission an external trainer. Remember that the trainer may well charge you for this time. Budget accordingly.

■ *What areas do you want to cover in the debriefing?*
You should be clear about this before you commission the trainer. From the commissioning organisation's point of view, debriefing is important to get the maximum value out of a training event.

Other areas which might usefully be covered in the debriefing session include:

– The trainer's views about the extent to which planned outcomes were achieved.

– Successful and unsuccessful aspects of the training event and the trainer's views on the reasons for these.

– Critical incidents which the trainer felt were particularly significant during the training event.

– Particular issues which were left unresolved at the end of the event.

– Any unintended outcomes from the training event.

– Potential areas for further training which were identified either by participants or the external trainer themselves.

– Suggestions from the trainer about how a similar event in the future might be improved.

– The trainer's views about the commissioning process.

– What the trainer wants from the debriefing session.

**Checklist 4.6 contd…**

Trainers will vary in the degree to which they wish to receive feedback about their own performance. This should, therefore, be negotiated with the trainer. However, you have a responsibility to participants in the trainer's future events to point out any major negative feedback arising from your own event. Feedback should be handled sensitively, and you will have to be explicit with both trainers and participants about confidentiality in any evaluation form. Since there is little reason why an external trainer needs to know which participant made which comment, a good rule of thumb is for the person who commissions the training to summarise the feedback and pass this on to the trainer in an unattributable form.

Trainers rarely get feedback when things go well. To avoid the difficulties inherent in assuming that 'no news is good news', you should also pass on positive comments about the trainer's performance. As a trainer yourself, you will know how it feels when you are told that you have done something well. Why deny that feeling to others?

**Notes:**

84

**So, what is this thing called electronic training or e-training?** This section perhaps ought to be entitled 'Work in progress' or 'Watch this space' since no-one can yet predict how far the use of the Internet for training purposes will expand. Or, possibly more importantly, which directions and forms it will take. Internet training sites such as: www.trainingzone.co.uk have hosted considerable debates and examples of the use of e-conferencing and e-learning, but in reality the whole area is still in its infancy, and only a relatively few organisations have taken the plunge into putting all their 'training eggs' into this particular basket.

Gilly Salmon is one of the UK's foremost proponents of e-learning, and is chair of the Open University Business School's online Professional Certificate in Management. She has developed a programme of what she calls **e-tivities**, which are activities for shared and individual learning, run by an e-moderator for a group of learners. Salmon, further defines e-tivities as **online active and inter-active learning**. Her book *e-tivities* is an informative read on the subject and about as up-to-date as you can currently get. But even she admits that the 'state of play' is not clear:

> *Instead of the predicted replacement of education by electronic means, we witness a web of educational providers, using ever more sophisticated networked technologies, constantly repositioning themselves in a slippery market place.*

And later, she adds:

> *… every tutor is still challenged to make interaction and participation online work really well in the service of learning objectives and outcomes.*

If ever there was a learning curve, this is one, and any of us considering using the Internet to provide training must take a deep breath, and be prepared to be flexible, patient and learn along with their students.

## The potential of e-training and e-learning

Getting people into one place at the same time is the essence of organising the traditional training events described in this book so far. It is often very time-consuming and expensive to achieve, especially where those attending have to travel long distances and stay residentially at the venue. It is also the potential cause of possibly severe disruption in the people-services workplaces as staff troop off to training or conference events. However, frequently it is the interaction between delegates at an event which provides the greatest added value to an event – in itself often greater than any accreditation or certification of staff skills.

So, for me, e-training and e-learning provide **complementary** ways and means to providing learning and development opportunities for staff. In particular, because e-training does not take place in as Star-trekkies would say, the 'same place and time continuum', it means that it is inherently more flexible for meeting individual learning needs, at least in terms of time. My main concern is that organisations might try to use e-learning as a cheap alternative to existing methods of running training events, rather than as a complementary set of tools. I don't think that it can replace real-time human interaction, but having said that, I believe that it can and will provide some new and innovative learning opportunities for training.

I would assume that all trainers in the 2000s use e-mail and have some experience of using the Internet and visiting web sites. The organisation of e-training is a natural extension of using e-mailing. With e-mail you can send a letter to one person, or copy it to a group of people. Words and blocks of words can be cut and pasted into new documents, and whole files and images can be attached to e-mails, ready for saving and opening by the recipients. Discussion groups and forums build on the e-mail function, for instance, I am a member of Trav-net which links together academics, workers, Gypsies and travellers in the UK and beyond. Every note that any of us send to the central hub e-mail address is re-sent to all the list members. Our list master, Colin Clark, in the Department of Social Policy at Newcastle University, moderates the exchanges and ensures that members observe a set of not too onerous rules regarding 'netiquette'. We can also send individual responses to any particular member. In essence it is an *informal* training network which enables us to:

- Exchange information about events, news, training and new publications.
- Share news reports in the media concerning Gypsies and travellers.
- Help to co-ordinate services for travellers in areas such as education, health and legal representation.
- Offer opinions and views on significant matters whether it is *Roma* in eastern europe, the annual holocaust day, or historical and linguistic issues.
- Campaign for and on behalf of travellers' rights.

As can be seen from this list, the potential range of information exchanged is very considerable. One person may seek to link their traveller education team in the north of England with others across the UK and beyond. Another may request help to prevent the eviction of a Gypsy site. Some use the group as a support network for international solidarity between nomadic groups.

The technology to run such a group is neither expensive nor too formidably complicated, at least at the basic level of operation. Because we do not sign on at any particular time of day or night, or with any particular regularity it is completely **asynchronous** – meaning interaction between list members takes place over time. This means that as a simple example of an e-training forum it is:

- Flexible.
- Modifiable.
- Relatively easy to organise and moderate.
- Allows learners and participants to participate at their own speed and at times which suit them – which makes it potentially very 'learner-centred'.
- Brings with it some measure of egalitarianism between members (all are teachers and learners).

- Offers some positive aspects of *not* being in the same place at the same time.
- Overcomes physical barriers for people with disabilities, limited time, lack of finances to attend events or meet together.

However, there are also some pitfalls and potential problems and resistances. These include:

- Learning to use the medium and any software.
- Fear of the unknown.
- Loss of actual human contact.
- Some set-up costs and, if this is translated from the above example into a more elaborate training course or programme, then there may be a considerable cost in time and preparation of materials.
- e-training needs patient and consistent moderation and support for its community.
- In a training course, quality assurance of the material and tuition or moderation may present a problem.
- Learning the codes of acceptable e-behaviour.

Of course, an e-event does not have to be asynchronous. Using web-cams (cameras) and microphones it is possible to set up an e-conferencing event, session or meeting in **synchronous** time. This has been possible for some years using 'old technology' telephones, linking up a group of people based in different locations. I've only been personally involved in a couple of examples where we linked up people who couldn't actually appear at a conference, but who were wanted to make short presentations and engage in the related discussion. It worked up to a point. The main problems seemed to be in the way that it broke the flow of proceedings, and the lack of 'being there' caused some misunderstandings which don't occur if you can judge body language and make eye contact between participants. The technical challenges of this sort of event are far greater than for simple e-mail exchanges, and it relies on a lot more co-ordination and commitment from everyone that is involved.

## Implementing e-learning and e-training

As yet I haven't taken the plunge and tried to organise a **virtual training event**. However, I can envisage that it would actually be possible to organise the planning of an event through the establishment of a simple **e-planning group**. Once the programme for the event has been thoroughly debated by the e-planning group, a simple event or sequence could be organised. If the form of the event planned and implemented over the Internet was monitored properly this module could then be replicated very easily, which would make it potentially ideal for what Gilly Salmon calls **learning cohorts**. Qantas Airlines use these cohort groups of staff joining their modular training programme. Maybe next year it will be one of the geographically spread social work departments, such as Strathclyde Region!

What seems to be true of this new era of training possibilities is that it can be very useful for:

- Sharing and constructing knowledge through an interactive process of all the participants.
- Making the most of participants' prior experience, skills and learning.
- Providing a range of levels for engagement.
- Problem solving and decision-making.
- Allowing learners a flexible pace for their learning.
- Implementing a structured developmental learning package for staff members.

In a number of my own training sessions, particularly with teams, I have used a range of consensus and decision-making techniques in order to get everyone in a particular group to:

- Get involved.
- Become a stakeholder in decisions.
- Set priorities for specific work activities (at the micro level) and for the agency (at the macro level).

This sort of exercise is ideally suited for using within any e-learning group. Checklist 5.1 (see page 89) is a possible example that could be easily modified to suit the training needs of any group. I have adapted it from a sequence I use called the *Consensus Game, Take Five*, and one Salmon cites from Sivasailam 'Thiagi' Thiagarajan's web site: www.thiagi.com. It is particularly useful for getting a group of staff members to design a mission statement or manifesto for action.

## Stages in the e-learning process

The most important thing to remember in e-learning is that the learning process should be both *designed* and *facilitated* in order to ease participants into a new medium of learning. It should also use the previous experience – sometimes called the **prior learning** of participants – as a building block in the development process.

Salmon describes these as being embodied in five stages of **structured learning processes**. However, in the sorts of training and knowledge development that the people-services would wish to engage in, this might translate into something like Checklist 5.2 (see page 90).

If you want to learn more about Gilly Salmon's work and experience with e-tivities, log onto: www.e-tivities.com

# Checklist 5.1: Owning priorities

Invite everyone involved in the group to engage in the following staged activity:

1.  Ask everyone to submit three suggestions for what services or facilities they would like to improve for their client group.

2.  The moderator cuts and pastes these into one list, combining any that are similar.

3.  The new list is shared with everyone and each person can use five votes for suggestions on the list according to what they would wish to prioritise. They can give all five votes to one item or spread them across the list.

4.  The moderator works out the result of this vote but does not share it with the group at this stage.

5.  The moderator re-sends the list from stage 3, this time asking participants to use five votes according to how they think that the entire group would have voted.

6.  The moderator then works out the results of stage 5 voting, and shares back the results of the two priority lists, selected in stages 3 and 5. The results may show some interesting differences between how individuals voted (wishful thinking) and how they think that the group as a whole prioritised the best ways of improving services (group cohesion/consensus). The moderator would then facilitate a discussion on the outcomes of the voting and help to determine a set of priorities if appropriate and desired.

# Checklist 5.2: Model of the five stages of a structured learning process

1. **A gateway to learning:** participants learn about using the Internet system and how they will be involved with the rest of the learning group or community and their facilitator. At this stage participants are largely being reactive and gaining motivation from the facilitator.

2. **Joining in:** participants start to 'meet' and 'greet' each other. They establish online identities and begin to participate in a proactive way.

3. **Information and knowledge exchange:** participants share ideas, viewpoints and information.

4. **Tackling tasks and group working:** participants begin to work collaboratively and co-operate on task solving and start to use the online environment to work in the e-environment as a group as well as individually.

5. **Further developments:** participants have gained a mutual understanding and maturity and can take on a range of new tasks and may mentor new people into the learning community.

# Section 6 — Equipment and Materials

The range of possible **audio-visual aids** and **equipment** that can be used by trainers and facilitators is now vast. This makes the task facing planning co-ordinators more complex than ever. Added to these equipment requirements are the materials and equipment that are needed for each small group session or workshop, materials for conference packs and, in some cases, materials for a post-conference report, or during-the-conference newspaper. The resource implications mean that the task of gathering equipment will probably be spread among a number of people, notably:

- the conference or event organisers
- workshop or session facilitators
- the venue management team and in particular their technicians
- outside specialist services and suppliers

## Potential equipment and materials

The range of possible equipment needs is almost limitless. In Checklist 6.1 (see page 96) I have listed some of the items I had to help assemble for a conference of 250, which operated on the basis of a mixture of plenary inputs and eight concurrent workshops. It may give organisers some ideas of a potential 'shopping list' of requirements. You may wish to use it for crossing out items not needed and adding others in as required. It is worth using in conjunction with the organisers' toolkit (Checklist 3.4) included in Section 3.

When you are looking through the range of available equipment, it will quickly become obvious that the sky literally is the limit and that *en route* you could hire fog, dry ice, flowers, marquees and the odd few specialists in pyrotechnics! Different types of event will have different equipment needs. If you are thinking of planning some kind of media launch, perhaps to promote the establishment of a new voluntary organisation, or to heighten the profile of an area of work, homelessness, for instance, the equipment needs and possibly the use of specialist service providers may become imperative. Starvision-type screens, on to which the image of your speakers can be back-projected, special stage sets, autocue and prompt equipment can all be obtained – at a price.

## Possible services and facilities required

In the corporate world, commercial conferences and product launches are most definitely big business. Checklist 6.2 (see page 97) is a list of classifications, reprinted courtesy of *The Corporate Event Services* annual guide (www.cesbook.co.uk). It gives a very clear picture of the diversity of services and facilities which are on offer and which might be required by conference and training event organisers.

# Audio-visual options

Sometimes it is easy to fall into the trap of using resources you have always used, without considering all the options available. I would suggest you make yourself a checklist with the various headings of equipment you might need and then write down the factors to consider and the choices you have. In Checklist 6.3 (see page 100), I have started off the process, but your event may have particular needs, so fill your own boxes as well.

Whenever presentations are to be made using audio-visual equipment, make sure that the equipment is checked thoroughly, if possible with the help of a skilled technician. In addition to the equipment itself, it is worth making sure that connections to the Internet, other equipment, spare bulbs, fuses, overhead projection pens, tapes and power cables are at hand and also checked to be working.

These aids really do make presentations more interesting, but, particularly with computers and video, organisers must try to produce and use the highest quality production techniques available. All film and video presentations tend to be judged by audiences against professional standards. In the people-services there is perhaps more willingness to accept videos that are 'fly on the wall' representations of real life, but a bad video or PowerPoint presentation can be even more embarrassing than a bad speaker, who will always evoke a measure of sympathy.

When used effectively, previously produced training videos, computer presentations, films and audio tapes can provide:

- useful slices of 'reality'
- improved presentation quality
- a greater variety of styles and images

and can save time and trouble for presenters when a training package has to be frequently repeated.

There may also be special requirements in presentations, such as the provision of a lectern, prompt-boards, black-outs, dimming of lights, Internet and large screen link and background music. Organisers must try to plan for as many eventualities as they can, and test out each piece of equipment in advance.

# Handouts

The main materials used in most training events are in the written, photocopied form. Participants often like something they can read and consider in their own time, either before a presentation or afterwards when they have returned to base. Many 'handouts' distributed before, or at, conferences are dreadful. They look to be hurriedly produced, illegible, badly thought out and presented, and generally they detract from the quality of the training. When producing handouts, training organisers must consider:

- layout and presentation quality
- language and style
- appropriateness for the audience
- objectives (e.g. do they inform, train, alter attitudes, etc.)
- length
- how they are to be used

Improvements in presentation quality will almost inevitably improve communication and increase the effectiveness of training inputs. With the wider availability of Word and DTP packages as well as good quality printers in mono and colour, there really isn't much excuse for badly produced handouts.

## Badges and signs

**Badges** for participants do help individuals who are initially unfamiliar with one another to 'put names to faces and organisations'. There are various ways of having badges made up and these will have differing cost implications. The usual information to include will be the name of the person and the organisation they are from. Some events also put in the 'position' held by the individual. To maintain uniformity on the badges, it is best for the organisers to write or type out the badges in advance, but, if time is short, or if the names of participants are uncertain, it is quite appropriate to ask participants to write out their own badge. Check in advance which types of pen will write on the badge surface!

The simplest badges are made from stick-on labels, but these fall off easily, tend to damage some types of clothes, and should only be considered in an emergency; round card badges with a safety pin on the back are cheap and cheerful and often come in day-glo colours as well as in white card. The next cheapest options are badges of card which have a plastic protective sleeve. Metal button badges made on a special badge-making machine provide more permanent badges and look quite nice. Finally there are a range of specialist firms who can custom make badges in all sorts of styles, including plastic and enamel. (Try, for instance, listings from *The Corporate Event Services* guide, which offers a number of firms who specialise in making signs.) With badges, signs, and conference newsletters and reports, remember it may be possible to obtain sponsorship to keep costs down.

**Signs** are almost always a must for any event. Initially they are required to direct participants to the event and these can be hand-made, or it is possible to negotiate special signs for large-scale events with the main motoring organisations, the RAC and the AA. When making signs for outdoor use, ensure that they are:

- Large enough to be legible at a sufficient distance not to cause a hazard to drivers.
- Waterproof.
- Sited at the correct road intersections.
- Showing correct, simple information and arrows.

Much the same is true of **indoor signs**: there are a number of uses for them. This includes:

- Indicating where different functions take place.
- Directing participants with arrows and perhaps colour codes.
- Identifying workshop rooms with colour codes or numbers.
- If not already obvious, identifying communal areas such as the dining area, plenary room or conference suite, bar, games room, office, etc.

In the planning stages, the organisers should work out where signs will be required, which way round arrows should point, and then they should make these signs up as part of the preparation process. It is often worth checking with the venue management regarding the use of signs, since they may already have some or, they may not like you super-gluing or nailing them to real oak doors!

## Conference newspapers, newsletters, reports

At a number of conferences and training events I have helped organise, quite a lot of effort has gone into making a daily **news sheet** available. This has advantages in giving all the participants information on sessions they couldn't attend and provides some basic report-back information to take away from the event and back to the workplace. It can also form part of the basis for a fuller, more professional **conference report**. And, for those involved and for those who receive it, it can be the source of a lot of fun and involvement!

If you are considering organising a newsletter, it will probably require about three people to co-ordinate it. Ideally, workshop leaders, rapporteurs, and speakers will all have material about their sessions available for passing on to the editorial group. Otherwise, the newsletter or newspaper reporters will have to chase round workshops while they are in progress, or catch the facilitators afterwards and conduct quick interviews about what went on.

To run a newspaper, some form of printing equipment, usually a photocopier is required, and a computer with software such as Word, to type the material and possibly scan or input photos into. You will also need paper, toner, ink, etc., maybe a stapler and staples, pens, ruler, glue and perhaps some means of obtaining photos for reproduction. This would provide the very basic equipment. The tasks involved are: writing, editing, typing, design and illustration, photography, and photocopying and collating. Then there is distribution around the conference hall or breakfast tables!

A lively and varied newspaper can be a focal point for debate, can add an element of humour to the event, and it does make the task of producing a final report on the event much easier.

Where a **conference report** is going to be produced, this needs to be costed in advance and built into the expenditure for the event. Sometimes outside assistance will have to be bought in since it is a substantial task. In addition to the tasks outlined for a conference newsletter, it is usually important to ensure that sessions are tape-recorded, or that full versions of keynote speeches are available to the report editor. Later transcription of speeches is very time consuming and laborious, so try for written copies, even if they are handwritten and a bit scruffy.

Photos become very important to enable the final report to look professional and well presented. With cheaper and more foolproof cameras, including those of digital quality, on the market, many more participants will be 'flashing' at the event and, with a bit of forward planning, can probably be involved in the production process. Conference reports may also require professional design, typesetting and printing, so this should be looked at in advance and quotes obtained. Try to set a limit to the likely size of the intended report, and this will provide boundaries for the editorial and production team to work within.

# Checklist 6.1: Potential equipment and materials

### Before the event
- Conference packs with a variety of handouts including different papers from workshops.
- Transport from station to venue: one mini-bus; one coach.
- Transport for equipment to venue.

### For registration
- Name badges for all participants.

### Main hall
- Six microphones.
- PA system.
- Video player.
- Six TV monitors sited on the walls of the auditorium.
- Acoustic panels to improve sound.
- Overhead projection system.
- Tape-slide player.
- Tape-recorder (mini-disc type) with high gain microphone.
- Video camera.
- Six glasses and water.
- Various handouts.

### Workshops
- Four computers.
- Photocopier.
- Three OHPs in concurrent use.
- Two video players.
- DVD player.
- Eight flip chart stands and paper and pens.
- Tape-slide player.
- Flowers and plants.
- Banner for conference and sponsors.
- Various handouts and equipment for exercises, games and simulations.

### Exhibition/market place
- 48 trestle-tables.
- 80 chairs.
- LIghts for 24 exhibitors' stands.
- Power leads and multiple sockets.
- Display stands for 12 stands.
- Two purpose-made display stands designed for the host organisation.
- Flowers and plants.

### Entertainment
- 1000 watt sound system for bass, lead, rhythm guitars, drums and three vocal microphones.
- Piano.
- Disco unit and DJ lighting rig for stage.
- FIlm projection equipment.
- Two entertainment films.

### General use
- Polaroid camera and films.
- 35mm camera and films.
- Digital camera and flash card.
- Computer, scanner and printer with software for editing digital images.
- Six clip-boards.
- Pens.
- Dictaphone.
- Everything else on the toolkit list (Checklist 3.4).

# Checklist 6.2: List of classifications

activity organisers
address labels
after dinner speakers
air and sea freighting
air charter
air conditioning/heating
associations
audience response
audio post production
audio visual (AV) equipment hire
AV equipment sale
AV manufacturing
AV presentation graphics
AV production
AV programming
AV recruitment
AV services
backdrops
badges and registration systems
balloons
banners
banqueting furniture
barriers
bars
blinds
booking agencies
bunting
car hire/chauffeur
car parking
carpet tiles
carpets
casinos
catering
catering equipment
catwalks
celebrities/entertainment agents
chauffeur drive/limousines
childcare
choreographers
coaches
communications
composers
computer graphics
computer hire
computer software
conference and event production

conference and event technical staging
conference coaches
conference furniture
conference microphones
conference organisers
conference production companies
conference production managers
conference recording
conference sets
conference staff
conference transcription
contact lists
convention bureaux
corporate activity organisers
corporate hospitality companies
costumes
crèche facilities
crewing services
cue lights
curtains
dance floors
dancers
data projection
decorations (floral)
demonstrators
discos and karaoke
display (large screen)
drapes
editing
electrics
electronic voting systems
entertainment agents
equipment cases
equipment manufacture and sale
equipment repair and maintenance
event catering
event management
event organisers
event passes and laminates
event software
event websites
exhibition graphics
exhibition halls
exhibition organisers
exhibition staff
exhibition stands

→

**Checklist 6.2 contd...**

exhibition units (mobile)
exhibition websites
fence hire/barriers
film and TV studios
finders of venues
fire protection
fireworks
flags and banners
flight cases
floor coverings
florists/floral displays
flying effects
freezers
freighting and forwarding
furniture hire/contractors
furniture sale
game-show equipment
game-show organisers
generators/power distribution
giant video screens
grandstands
high power projection
hospitality companies
hotels
inflatables/balloons
installation services
insurance
international support services
internet services
interpreters
interpreting equipment
laminates
large screen display
lasers
LED projectors
leisure equipment hire
lighting design and hire
limousines
logos
magicians
mailing list rental
manufacturing
marquees/temporary structures
merchandising
mobile exhibition units
mobile kitchens
mobile phone rentals

mobile refrigeration
mobile showers
mobile toilets
model makers
models
modular exhibition stands
moving lights
multimedia
music
music booking agents
music composers
office equipment
outdoor event services
outside broadcast units
overseas support services
PA hire
parking
participation events
party organisers
personalities
photographers (location)
plasma screens
portable exhibition units
portable sets
portable structures
post production (audio and video)
power distribution
presentation companies
presentation graphics
product launch production
production companies (conference)
production companies (video)
production managers (conference)
production music libraries
professional drivers
projection (large screen)
projection screens
promotional merchandise
prompting equipment
prop and model makers
prop hire
push to talk
pyrotechnics
quiz organisers
quiz scoring systems
radio communications
radio microphone hire

**Checklist 6.2 contd...**

| | |
|---|---|
| ramps | touchscreens |
| recruitment | towers |
| refrigeration rental | town criers |
| registration systems | trade associations |
| repair and maintenance | transcription (conference) |
| rigging supply/servicing | translation |
| rigging/trussing | transport (limousines) |
| roadshows | transport (ramps) |
| roadsigns | transport (trucking) |
| rodeo bulls | transport air and sea freighting |
| ropes | transport air charter |
| rostra | transport coaches |
| satellite communications | travel agents |
| scenic projection | trucking |
| screen manufacturers | trussing |
| seating | universities/colleges |
| security | valet parking |
| set design and build | vehicle ramps |
| set designers | venue finders |
| show and event roadways | venues (specialist locations) |
| show organisers | venues (studios) |
| signs and graphics | venues (tourism offices) |
| simultaneous translation | venues (universities/colleges) |
| site services | video conferencing |
| sound systems design and hire | video equipment hire |
| speaker bureaux | video post production |
| speakers | video production companies |
| special effects | video walls |
| stage lighting | voice over agencies |
| stagecrew | voting |
| staging | walkie talkies |
| staging (conference) | waste clearance |
| starcloth | water effects |
| storage | webcasting |
| support services (international) | websites |
| T shirts, mugs etc. | wristbands |
| technical staging (conference) | |
| teleconferencing | |
| temperature control | |
| temporary roadways | |
| temporary structures | |
| tents | |
| theatres | |
| theme staging | |
| themed events | |
| tickets | |
| toilets | |

# Checklist 6.3: Equipment options

| Video | Still cameras | OHP and computers |
|---|---|---|
| Format: Digital, Super VHS, VHS, U-matic, Video 8, Video-disc | Digital<br>Single lens reflex<br>Rangefinder<br>Twin lens reflex<br>35 mm<br>Polaroid<br>Advance Photo System<br>Half frame<br>Medium format | Projection size |
| Recording speed | | Computer type PC/Mac |
| Computer link | | Operating systems |
| Interactive | | Software, e.g. Powerpoint |
| Screen size | | Angle and wattage for OHP |
| Video/DVD playback machines | Black and white or colour film stock | |
| Amplifier | Digital output and software for editing | |
| Monitor speakers | Prints or transparencies | |
| **Boards** | **Slide projectors** | **Media transfer** |
| Blackboard | Single load | Film to video |
| Whiteboard | Cassette | Photos or slides to video |
| Flip-chart | Carousel | Photos or slides to display boards |
| Magnetic board | Wattage and angle | |
| Paper and blu-tack | Tape-link | |
| Relevant pens | Dissolve/multi-unit | |
| **Recording** | | |
| Digital recorder | | |
| Cassette recorder | | |
| Dictaphone | | |
| Video camera | | |
| Stenographer | | |
| **Other** | | |

# Section 7   Evaluation and Follow-up

## How to evaluate

An area in which training events and conferences often fail is **evaluation**. There is no single way to evaluate 'success' or 'failure' of training, nor is an instant reaction necessarily an accurate reflection of impact. Most importantly, the evaluation of training must be seen as a process, not as a one-off activity. There is also the added complication of accreditation, where it is the participants who are first being 'evaluated' prior to any opportunity they have to comment on the skill training they have been on the receiving end of!

Getting comments and feedback on the subject of training is, at its simplest level, purely a matter of asking potential or actual participants, organisers, speakers and facilitators for their own opinions and views. The stages at which this dialogue can take place include:

- At the programme planning stage.
- At the stage of evaluating individual and agency training needs.
- During, and at the end of specific workshops or plenary sessions.
- At the conclusion of the training event, conference or course.
- In accredited learning, the particular event may be part of a process of evaluation or accreditation for the individual concerned.
- At some point after the event to allow for reflection and to measure the effectiveness of the training in changing practice.

These stages are not mutually exclusive. As a training organiser, you may opt to have evaluation built in to each stage of the training, or only try to evaluate the whole event. The nature, and the style of the event being run, will offer some indication as to the best type of evaluation tools to use. In this section of the book I have brought together a number of sample questionnaires and activities which gain feedback. The most frequently used methods for obtaining feedback include:

- Organising a feedback or response session in the final plenary.
- Asking for comments at the end of each individual session.
- Requesting written comments on the event as a whole and the individual sessions.
- Using questionnaires to solicit responses.
- Issuing a limited distribution, survey form, to a sample section of the participants.
- Conducting structured interviews with some of the participants after the event.
- Using repertory grids or semantic differential tables and comparative assessment techniques (don't panic, they're not too painful!)
- Through the organisers, comparing results with the original objectives and aims.
- Holding some sort of 'post-mortem' session, either just for the organisers or including at least some of the participants – this might utilise focus groups.

Directly linked to the above, organisers have to ask themselves:

*Why evaluate the event and its component parts?*

… which naturally leads to a consideration of:

*What were the expected outcomes?*

*Have they been achieved?*

Some of the 'answers' to these questions will involve the performers, the speakers and workshop leaders, in a two-way process of making their own self-assessment of their own performances, and reflecting on the evaluation and comments offered by others. So, it is necessary to construct different sets of evaluation material for different groups. In more scientific settings, the test of evaluation methods for training is assessed according to its reliability and validity. This is not always easy in the context of people-work training, but it should be possible to obtain feedback on:

- The content, methods and styles used for inputs and the performance of facilitators.
- The programme design.
- Aspects of the administration such as the registration, catering and entertainment.
- Accommodation.
- The venue and its location.
- Travel arrangements.
- Exhibition and market place.
- Relevance to the workplace.
- Potential for improving management and practice.
- Skills, knowledge and information obtained at the event.
- What went 'right' and 'wrong' – lessons learned.
- How far 'aims' were met.
- Future training requirements: personal and professional expectations.

## Why evaluate?

Organisers will reach their own conclusions on this question, but I would suggest that evaluation and feedback are critical in:

- Analysing the effectiveness of different trainers and training methods and styles.
- Enabling modifications and changes in future training to take place.
- Assessing the quality and value-for-money of training.
- Identifying skill acquisition and 'gaps' in present skills.
- Monitoring the relevance and practical application of training to the workplace.

Some events will have entirely different aims. Their success might be evaluated on criteria which relate to factors such as association membership level, the creation of a new pressure group, or the development or acceptance of certain policies.

# Workplace assessment, accreditation and appraisal

In people-work, the system of **credit accumulation transfer**, both in NVQs and in other programmes of training has begun to improve the skills and knowledge of many staff, who previously had few chances to access 'accredited' training. It should also lead to less distinction between what has previously been seen as 'academic' (high status) learning, and 'experiential' learning (hitherto lower status), which validates on-the-job and individual knowledge-base of staff. Where staff are to be involved as **workplace assessors**, they need to make sure that they have:

- Clearly explained the basis for assessment.
- Offered examples of 'best practice' and incorrect or inefficient methods.
- Enabled staff to participate in the process and develop personal ownership and responsibility for their training and professional development.
- Involved participants in the assessment or evaluation procedure.
- Tried to use assessment as an ongoing process to improve motivation, and service delivery.

Watts, Pickles and Miller in *Social Care Professional Development* highlighted some of the problematic areas in developing means for evaluating successful **professional development systems**:

- *Does the method provide qualitative or quantitative data, or both?*
- *Is it reliable? Would it provide similar information on a subsequent occasion when measuring the same situation?*
- *Is it a valid measure? Does it measure what it sets out to measure?*
- *How practical is it? How easy is it to use?*
- *How much time is needed by the co-ordinator? And by the respondents?*
- *How much detail can it provide? How specific is it?*
- *How good is it at encouraging open and honest responses from respondents?*
- *How flexible is it? Does it allow follow-up in other related areas as needed?*

In a later book, *Performance Appraisal*, Hope and Pickles examined how staff development and performance appraisal relate to one another. The avoidance of worries about **'punishment and victimisation'** is central to their model of appraisal. Among their findings they underlined the need for organisations to become **learning organisations**, where the whole organisation is geared up to facilitate the learning of all its members, both about their own performance and skills, but also about changes in the professions, communities and society around them. Within such a learning organisation, the authors Hope and Pickles contend that non-hierarchical means of appraisal can be employed in order to:

- Develop individual staff capacity and skills.
- Avoid aggressive, discriminatory or unsupportive practices.
- Enhance job satisfaction.
- Encourage participative policy and practice.
- Develop positive partnerships both within and outside the organisation.

# Training needs assessment

To build on the implications of the points raised above on appraisal and assessment of training and individual performance, it can be seen that evaluating training and the process of 'being trained' is extremely complex. Even if it wasn't difficult enough, it is inevitably made more complicated – and more rewarding – if it is participative and co-operative, involving all the participants. And, at the commencement of this process, **training needs** must be examined as part of this **partnership** between the trainer and the person going to be trained.

I have personally been at the receiving end of performance appraisal, as well as being a so-called **appraiser**. In too many cases, the process of staff development does not seem to be 'interactive' at all. Instead it can appear to be dehumanised, mechanistic and organisationally biased, and personally 'disempowering'. I can remember being asked by my appraiser:

> How do you think you've achieved in the last six months relative to corporate GP targets?

OK, at the time I was a publishing manager for the publishers, Longman, but even so, it hardly seemed likely to improve my personal motivation. I wanted to help commission and publish useful books for social welfare staff, not just be judged according to gross profits.

Our professional needs are a peculiar blend of necessity and luxury. 'Be all you can be' has been used as the promotional catch-phrase of health education in Scotland, and it is a suitable aim for training as well. Every individual should be motivated to be all they can be. Training, if organised on the basis of collaboration and needs, can be the major enabling strategy for helping individuals to make the most of their work-related lives.

Sometimes the language of training makes this more difficult rather than easier. Potential trainees are frightened off from being trained because courses seem 'alien', too academic and not related to their lives. The buzz words in training are not really helping to resolve this dilemma. Looking through training documents is frequently like moving to another planet, and having to learn a new language and code of behaviour. Courses and events sound as though they have been contrived by a committee designing camels, rather than as the means to improve an individual's skills. Whilst the content and approaches used in courses with titles such as *Human resource strategies*, *Critical enabling knowledge*, *Operations research*, *Corporate planning*, *Interactive learning*, *Action-centred learning* and *Neuro-linguistic programming* may be useful, as has been suggested elsewhere in this book, in themselves the titles do little to facilitate learning. However useful these types of titles are to us as trainers, we must look consistently at the effect that language has on the potential trainee. All too often it creates fear and produces barriers to being trained. Checklist 7.1 (see page 108) is a modest attempt to overcome that block. Rather than a 'tool' for management, or a means of assessment, this questionnaire is structured as a form of communication. Training should always be 'person-centred', and listening to the views of the potential receivers of training is at the core of the work.

# Feedback techniques

The evaluation of training is essentially a process whereby the original objectives for a training event are scrutinised, progress is evaluated, and then new objectives for further training can be established. There is a natural curve of participant response to training which looks like a switchback through time (see Fig. 7.1).

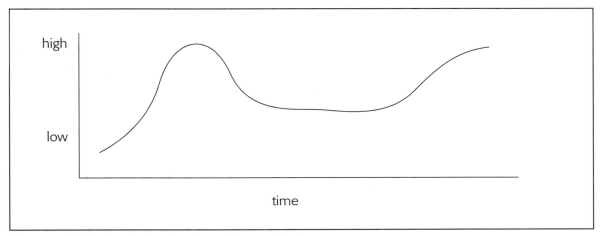

**Figure 7.1: Natural response curve to training inputs**

This being the case, don't get too despondent if not all your training efforts appear to be paying immediate dividends.

## *Setting objectives*

One sample grid which might be modified to analyse the effectiveness of the training you are providing is shown in Checklist 7.2 (see page 109). You may wish to fill in the grid with your own particular information at each stage: setting objectives for each area of input, comments at evaluation stage and re-definition of objectives following the evaluation.

The grid may be worth using with different groups who are or have been involved in a training event, since the perceptions of the organisers, trainers, managers and basic grade staff could, for instance, all vary.

## *Repertory grids*

These are frequently used in surveys and questionnaires, where the researchers want measurable, what is called 'quantifiable' responses to particular questions and situations.

Checklists 7.3 (see page 110) and 7.4 (page 111) are two simple examples I have used. They can take a bit of work in analysing, and like all survey techniques there is always a question of the 'research effect', where the person responds in the ways they do, just because they are 'being researched'. Working with children for much of my life, I am clear that responses to questions must be carefully considered before jumping to conclusions. Adults undergoing any form of training can also offer the answers they think the organisers want to hear, or, conversely be 'bloody minded' and negative for the sake of causing some mayhem.

Repertory grids ask a sequence of questions which require grading, usually from 0 to 5, or 0 to 10, or in percentages 0% to 100%, or alphabetic, A to E (high to low value). The choices offer the respondents the opportunity to give a response which is more complex than just a yes or no answer. Most grids are based on a scale linked to criteria such as *useless* (0) to *very useful* (5), or *low value* (0) to *high value* (10). The scales you use are a matter of choice. In both of my examples there are also open-ended questions that allow for the participants to respond flexibly to the form.

### Semantic differential questionnaires

These offer the respondent the choice between two variables in a rather different way to repertory grids. The example in Checklist 7.5 (see page 112) might be used to obtain a response to training that was intended to alter attitudes.

This example is very simple, but you might wish to mix up the positive and negative answers to the right and left of the grid.

### Comparative assessment technique

A rather more unusual device is the **comparative assessment technique**, which, if properly analysed, can help to evaluate what participants really think about subjects. However, you do need to be very careful to construct a grid that is appropriate and meaningful for the participants. The idea is to ask for a response which compares each variable in term of the **comparative importance** for the respondent.

So, for instance, in Checklist 7.6 (see page 113), if you think A is more important than B, you fill in A into the top left-hand box.

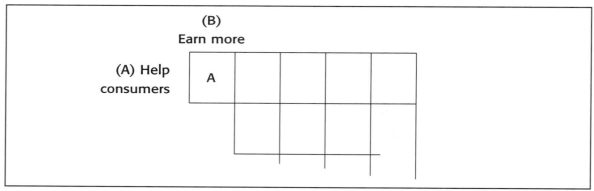

Figure 7.2

### Training questionnaire for workshop leaders

Finally, in Checklist 7.7 (see page 114), I have reproduced one example of a training questionnaire for workshop leaders/facilitators. This could easily be modified for use with speakers giving plenary inputs. The aim is to make training an ongoing concern and to:

- Learn from successes and mistakes.
- Modify and amend the contents and styles of presentation, as necessary.
- Be flexible.
- Try to meet the needs of individuals as well as organisations and employers.

# And finally ...

... as a training organiser, do try to enjoy what you are doing. Without the element of fun, most training is less relevant and more pedestrian. The inputs at training events and in conferences do not have to be boring. Hopefully, some of the contents of this book may make your next event just a bit more varied, participative and interesting. You might even make a profit, if that is your intention. Have fun, and very good luck!

**Alan Dearling**
Lyme Regis, Dorset

## Checklist 7.1: Training needs assessment

This short questionnaire has been designed to help you receive training which will help you in your work, now and in the future. We will make every effort to respond positively to your ideas and organise training opportunities which meet your needs and help to increase your skills.

In your work, what do you feel most confident doing?

What areas of work worry you?

What sort of training do you think might help you overcome these worries?

In an absolutely ideal world, what would you like to work at?

Are there any other skills or knowledge you would like to learn? What?

Are there any problems at work at present which in any way prevent you doing your best in your job?

What could be done to overcome these problems?

Thank you for taking the time to fill in this questionnaire. You may add your name if you wish. The contents will be treated in confidence and will only be discussed with you directly and not with anyone else.

# Checklist 7.2: Training input effectiveness and objectives

|  | Objectives ➔ | Evaluation ➔ | New Objectives ➔ |
|---|---|---|---|
| **TRAINING PROCESS**<br>Content, style and methods. |  |  |  |
| **KNOWLEDGE ACQUISITION**<br>Acquisition of skills, knowledge or new attitudes. |  |  |  |
| **SKILL APPLICATION**<br>Changes in practice and management. |  |  |  |
| **ORGANISATIONAL BENEFITS**<br>Costs/benefits. |  |  |  |

# Checklist 7.3: Participant evaluation sheet – example 1

*(Ring the appropriate response to each question)*

Name of event .................................................................................................................................................

|                                                                            | High |   |   |   | Low |
| -------------------------------------------------------------------------- | ---- | - | - | - | --- |
| Was the event relevant to your work?                                       | 5    | 4 | 3 | 2 | 1   |

Any comments? ...............................................................................................................................

| Were the main speeches interesting and useful for you? | 5 | 4 | 3 | 2 | 1 |
|---|---|---|---|---|---|

Any specific comments? ...............................................................................................................

| Was the balance between participation and listening acceptable? | 5 | 4 | 3 | 2 | 1 |
|---|---|---|---|---|---|

Ideas for how it could be improved ........................................................................................

| Was the event well organised? | 5 | 4 | 3 | 2 | 1 |
|---|---|---|---|---|---|

Ideas for improvements? ............................................................................................................

| What did you think of the workshops? | 5 | 4 | 3 | 2 | 1 |
|---|---|---|---|---|---|

Any particular comments? ...........................................................................................................

| How would you score the event overall? | 5 | 4 | 3 | 2 | 1 |
|---|---|---|---|---|---|

Any other comments for the organisers (catering, accommodation, entertainment, etc.)

Name ............................................................    Organisation ..................................................................
*(It is optional to fill this part in)*

# Checklist 7.4: Participant evaluation sheet – example 2

The aims of the course were stated as: *(Insert course aims.)*

(1)

(2)

(3)

(4)

(5)

1.  Please indicate, by circling the appropriate letter, the degree to which the course, so far, has for you met the above objectives.

    |       | High |   |   |   | Low |
    |-------|------|---|---|---|-----|
    | (1)   | A    | B | C | D | E   |
    | (2)   | A    | B | C | D | E   |
    | (3)   | A    | B | C | D | E   |
    | (4)   | A    | B | C | D | E   |
    | (5)   | A    | B | C | D | E   |

    |                                                        | High |   |   |   | Low |
    |--------------------------------------------------------|------|---|---|---|-----|
    | 2. How much new knowledge have you gained?             | A    | B | C | D | E   |
    | 3. How enjoyable is the course?                        | A    | B | C | D | E   |
    | 4. Have you changed your attitude/views on the nature of the work? | A | B | C | D | E |
    | 5. How helpful have the information handouts been?     | A    | B | C | D | E   |
    | 6. Are the consultancy groups proving useful?          | A    | B | C | D | E   |
    | 7. What is your overall assessment of the course to date? | A | B | C | D | E |

8.  In your opinion, which sessions have been the  most successful? *(Please give reasons.)* ..................................................................................................

9.  Which sessions have been the least successful? *(Please give reasons.)* ..........................
    ..................................................................................................

10. Please indicate what you feel are the best features of the course? ...................................
    ..................................................................................................

11. Please indicate what you feel are the worst features of the course? ..................................
    ..................................................................................................

12. How might the course be improved? ...............................................................

## Checklist 7.5: Participant questionnaire – example 3 (semantic differential)

Would you say, as result of the training input, that you:

*(Mark your response with a cross along the line to indicate the degree to which you agree with the answer at one or other end of the grid line)*

| | | |
|---|---|---|
| Are more confident | I.........I..........I..........I..........I..........I | Are less confident |
| Understand the subject more | I.........I..........I..........I..........I..........I | Are no more knowledgeable |
| Have acquired new skills | I.........I..........I..........I..........I..........I | Are no more skilled |
| Are competent for the current task | I.........I..........I..........I..........I..........I | Are in need of further training |

# Checklist 7.6: Comparative assessment technique – example 4

Please choose the most important criteria for **you personally**; comparing each option with each other lettered option:

**Training should help me to:**

(For example if you think that *Earning more* (B) is more important than *Helping customers*, write **B** in the first box comparing A with B.)

|  | (B) | (C) | (D) | (E) | (F) = get promoted |
|---|---|---|---|---|---|
| Help consumers/ customers (A) |  |  |  |  |  |
| Earn more (B) |  |  |  |  |  |
| Move to a new job (C) |  |  |  |  |  |
| Be more efficient (D) |  |  |  |  |  |
| Save money (E) |  |  |  |  |  |

## Checklist 7.7: Training questionnaire for workshop leaders – example 5

What are your reactions to the conference as a whole? .................................................................

.................................................................................................................................................

How do you feel your workshop was received? ...........................................................................

.................................................................................................................................................

Are there ways in which we, as a group, could have offered you more support? ...................

.................................................................................................................................................

Are there specific ways in which the structure of the conference could have been improved?

.................................................................................................................................................

.................................................................................................................................................

What, for you, was the most successful aspect of the event? ...................................................

.................................................................................................................................................

What was the least successful aspect of the event? ...................................................................

.................................................................................................................................................

Are there any training needs for staff members that you feel the planning group should address itself to in the next 18 months? ..........................................................................................

.................................................................................................................................................

Are you planning any particular initiatives that you would like us to get involved with?

.................................................................................................................................................

.................................................................................................................................................

Name: ....................................................................................................................................

Position: .................................................................................................................................

Address: .................................................................................................................................

.................................................................................................................................................

Reference sources on 'training' are almost endless. They are also forever changing, evolving and moving. I have listed some of the organisations I'm aware of who are actively involved in people-work training and a number of the books, manuals and materials that I have used in my work. They may provide a starting point for looking further into the various facets of training work. However, some may also be out of print and only now available in specialist libraries.

## Resource and training agencies

A number of publishing firms produce high quality training materials. Some are in the commercial field; others are professional training organisations who also act as publishers. Among the leaders in this field are Gower, Kogan Page, Social Care Institute for Excellence (and National Institute for Social Work), Routledge, University Associates, Russell House Publishing, Longman, Ashgate; John Wiley, Pavilion, and the Open University.

Many organisations offer training and consultancy support in the broad area of the personal social services. Others offer Internet portals to a whole array of resources and organisations. They include:

**Social Science Information Gateway**, Institute for learning and research technology, University of Bristol, 8-10 Berkley Square, Bristol BS8 1HH. www.sosig.ac.uk

**Social Care Institute for Excellence**, 1st floor, Golding's House, 2 Hay's Lane, London SE1 2HB. www.scie.org.uk

**Social Care training** at the Department of Health. www.doh.uk/scg/training.htm

**School of Health and Social Welfare** at the Open University. www.open.ac.uk/shsw/

**Institute for Public Policy Research**. www.ippr.org.uk

**The Work Foundation**, Peter Runge House, 3 Carlton Terrace, London SW1 5DG. www.theworkfoundation.com

**Capita Learning and Development**, 17 Rochester Row, London SW1P 1LA. 0870 4000 1000

**Impact training**. www.impact-training.co.uk

**e-tivities** (Gilly Salmon). www.e-tivities.com

**The Training Zone**. www.trainingzone.co.uk

## Reference materials

As I've already suggested, some of these are quite old, out of print and may only be found in specialist libraries. Others have gone through a number of reprints and even publishers, so publication dates are not very helpful. Consequently they are alpha sorted by author/ editor and I have included publishers as known to me.

Baldwin, J. and Williams, H. *Active Learning: A Trainer's Guide*. Basil Blackwell.

Bee, F. and R. *Training Needs: Analysis and Evaluation*. CIPD.

Bird, M. *How to Make Your Training Pay*. Business Books.

Birkenbihl, M. *Train the Trainer*. Chartwell-Bratt.

Brandes, D. *The Gamesters Handbook*. Hutchinson.

Burke, W., Warner and Beckhard, R. *Conference Planning*. University Associates.

Caffarella, R. *Program Development and Evaluation Resource Book for Trainers*. John Wiley.

Cattermole, F. et al. *Managing Youth Services*. Longman.

Charney, C. and Conway, K. *The Trainer's Toolkit*. Amacom.

Clark, D. *Organising and Running Training Events*. National Extension College.

Corporate Event Publishing. *Corporate Event Services*. Corporate Event Publishing.

Daily Telegraph. *Conferences and Meetings: How to Set Up and Run*. Telegraph/Kogan Page.

Dearling, A. and Armstrong, H. *The New Youth Games Book*. Russell House Publishing.

Dearling, A. with Armstrong, H. *World Youth Games*. Russell House Publishing.

Dearling, A. *Effective Teambuilding in Social Welfare Organisations*. Russell House Publishing.

Douglas, R. et al. *Helping People to Work Together*. NISW.

Dynes, R. *Creative Games in Groupwork*. Winslow.

Firkin, P. *The Training Paper*. Advance.

Harris, M. *Training and Education for the Voluntary Sector*. LSE.

Heider, J. *The Tao of Leadership*. Wildwood.

Honey, P. and Mumford, A. *The Manual of Learning Styles*. Honey.

Hope, P. and Pickles, T. *Performance Appraisal*. Russell House Publishing.

Jolly, A. *Skills and Training Directory*. Kogan Page.

Klatt, B. *The Ultimate Training Workshop Handbook*. McGraw Hill.

Koch, H. *Training Manuals in TQM*. Pavilion.

Koch, H. *Total Quality Management in Health Care*. Longman.

Krempl, S. and Wayne Pace, R. *Training Across Multiple Locations*. Berrett Kochler.

Locke, T. *Conference Organisation: Hints and Tips*. NACRO.

Locke, T. *Running a Conference by Computer*. NACRO.

Morgan, G. *Imaginization*. Sage.

Nadler, L. and Nadler, Z. *The Conference Book*. Gulf.

Pedlar, M. *Action Learning in Practice*. Gower.

Pickles, T., Britton, B. and Armstrong, H. *Developing Training Skills*. Longman.

Priestley, P. et al. *Social Skills and Personal Problem Solving*. Tavistock.

Richter, L. *Training Needs: Assessment and Monitoring*. International Labour Office.

Rogers, A. *Recording and Reporting*. NAYC.

Salmon, G. *e-tivities: the Key to Active Online Learning*. Kogan Page

Seekings, D. *How to Organise Effective Conferences and Meetings*. Kogan Page.

Sheal, P. *How to Develop and Present Staff Training Courses*. Kogan Page.

Smith, M. *Organise*. NAYC.

Stimson, N. *How to Write and Prepare Training Materials*. Kogan Page.

Taylor, B. *Experiential Learning: A Framework for Group Skills*. Oasis.

Taylor, H. and Mears, A. *The Right Way to Conduct Meetings, Conferences and Discussions*. Paperfronts.

Thorne, K. and Mackey, D. *Everything About Training*. Kogan Page.

Turner, S. *Planning and Organising Business Functions*. Gower.

Watts, P., Pickles, T. and Miller, A. *Social Care Professional Development*. Longman.

Young, A. *The Manager's Handbook*. Sphere.